What people are saying:

"*Your Wild and Precious Life* is an enlightening and honest peek into the life of Coach Jesse Gros. Having worked with him, I can tell you he is a hard-ass of love; he holds you accountable to your vision and is warm and kind at the same time. Best of all, he would never expect you to fight for your dreams if he hadn't done it himself. You know when you meet someone who is truly living their gift? Jesse is that guy and this book will leave you feeling like you just walked out of one of his powerful sessions."

— Lynsey Dyer, Professional Skier - First Ascent™

"I do not give out praises often but you are very talented at what you do. I see this is your passion and you are lucky to be able to engage in that passion, have a positive effect on people and make a great living at it. You had a very positive effect on my life in such a short time and I am very grateful to you for that."

— Jack Bitton, CEO of The Bitton Group

"Jesse Gros has written a galvanizing book that is hard to put down. While there are hundreds of inspirational books, Jesse takes you on a riveting personal journey, beginning with his traditional youth and leading, through exciting and unexpected twists and turns, to his highly nontraditional approach to enjoying and celebrating life....he lives his vision which is powerful and life-enhancing. Jesse is a coach's coach."

— Peter G. Engler, Executive Coach

"Jesse Gros has emerged as an entertaining and very moving travel writer...and by travel, I mean the inner and outer journey all true spiritual adventurers take...if your own journeys are stalled, this book will set you flying."

— Steve Chandler, author of *Time Warrior*

"This book is a roadmap to your destiny. Jesse lovingly guides you back to your own inner compass so that your heartfelt dreams, rather than your fears and expectations, become what guides you...and impacts not only what you create but the very essence of your human experience."

— Christine Hassler M.A., Author of *20 Something, 20 Everything*

YOUR
WILD & PRECIOUS
LIFE

Adventures in Conscious Creation

*Jesse*Gros

LOS ANGELES, CALIFORNIA

*Jesse*Gros

Los Angeles, California
www.jessegros.com

Original Cover Concept: Alexandria Zech
Cover Design: Matt Hinrichs
Book Designer: Ruth Schwartz

Your Wild & Precious Life / Jesse Gros. -- 1st ed.
ISBN 978-0-9897093-0-9

This book is dedicated to the courageous clients I have worked with, who have walked away from security and comfort to follow the yearnings of their heart.

And...to my beloved Alexandria, who has stood by me over the past four years, supporting me, encouraging me and being the best teammate anyone could have.

Acknowledgements

Dalia Mama for always believing in me
Alexandria Zech for her unwavering love
Peter Gros for teaching me the art of story
Ron & Mary Hulnick for being amazing mentors
Steve Chandler for inspiring me to write this book
Johanna Jenkins for keeping me on track my 2nd year
Rich Litvin for inspiring me to can my first book idea
David Elliott for teaching me the power of breath
Deanna Danski for taking me to the pizza man
Lindsay Patterson for introducing me to USM
Carole Engler for her keen attention to detail
Karma & Sonam Sherpa for The Small World
Zen for being my loyal writing companion
Kim Reynolds for connecting me to Nepal
Sonia Stringer for believing since day one
Martha Beck for opening me up to myself
Blair Souder for inspiring me to go deep
Jenny Bengen for her fine editing work
Ruth Schwartz for her fine layout work
Monika Zands, my first writing partner
Peter Engler for paving the way

Contents

CONSCIOUS CREATION

LOOKING FORWARD – NEXT STEPS

ABOUT JESSE GROS

INTRODUCTION

I BELIEVE WE LEARN BEST THROUGH STORY. This book is a collection of stories about finding your path and the courage to follow it. It includes stories from my journey over the last twenty years, including leaving medicine, walking away from Corporate America and struggling to get out of my head and into my heart to follow my own path.

It includes stories about courageous clients I have coached and inspirational people I have met along the way.

You will meet Jill S. who left her career and became a National Geographic photographer; David Rollins, who raised $5 million to start his non-profit; and Briana who had a surprise life-changing discovery while on retreat in Peru.

I'll share with you my key learnings about how I built a thriving coaching and international retreat business in the middle of a recession, with no prior experience.

You will read travel stories from Nepal, India and around the world. I hesitated to include some of these stories in the book, but ultimately I decided to follow my own advice and "Show 'em your uglies."

Also included are very personal stories about healing from both my life and from clients who have graciously agreed to let me share their experiences.

This is a book about the inner and outer journey of life; it is about healing, growth and conscious creation.

Ultimately, this is a book about you – *your* life and *your* path.

In the words of Mary Oliver:

"Tell me, what is it you plan to do with your one wild and precious life?"

*All of the stories in this book are true, as I remember them. However, many of the names and personal details have been changed to ensure client confidentiality.

THE PATH

That path of your Wild and Precious Life is rarely a straight one. Just like this book, it is a collection of experiences that don't always fit neatly together. Our lives bounce around, jut right, shoot left and fall out from underneath us when we least expect it. So often we are led off track and we lose ourselves along the way; lost in other people, strangled by careers that don't fit us and smothered by the expectations of our culture, family and friends.

It takes a tremendous amount of heart to continually step off false paths and back into ourselves.

Your Dream Does Not Have an Expiration Date

A T 18 YEARS OLD, I had a clear vision of what I wanted to be. I imagined myself leading international retreats all over the world to places like Nepal and India. On those retreats, people would dive into the culture and themselves and leave transformed. I imagined myself up on stage inspiring a large crowd of people to follow their dreams. I saw myself working with coaching clients from all over the world. I would be traveling and taking their calls from wherever I wanted to be, unhindered by an office or physical work place. I wrote the entire thing down in my goals journal. I envisioned it all happening...

Then...

I spent the next 18 years doing almost everything but that.

Which begs the question:

"Why is it we resist the very things we want the most?"

My resistance was so strong, it kept me from realizing my vision for almost two decades.

And I had all kinds of great excuses, fears and seemingly legitimate reasons why I could not follow my dream. I even convinced myself for a while that I didn't know what I wanted to do. Rather than dive right in, I ended up taking the long, circuitous route instead:

- Studied psychology in college. (Not what I imagined.)
- Waited tables. (This is a hard way to make money.)
- Worked in a warehouse. (What the heck am I doing here?)
- Went to acting school. (I love this!)
- Wrote and directed children's plays. (So fun, but no money.)
- Taught wakeboarding. (Ditto).
- Worked with autistic children. (Started out as fun, proved to be exhausting.)
- Saved money to go back to school.
- Went back to school, took the Medical School Entrance Exam. (Worked like a dog.)
- Dropped out. (Freedom and poverty.)
- September 11th happened. (Life is short, screw "someday.")
- Worked for Anthony Robbins. (Check!)
- Saved money to travel the world for a year.
- Traveled the world. (Check!)
- Returned home with no job. (Bank account back to zero.)
- Substitute teacher in low-income schools. (What am I doing here?)
- Life coach for a minute, then quit. (I had one client.)
- Left it all to become an insurance adjuster for Hurricane Katrina. (Financial success.)
- Saved money to start a business.
- Went to graduate school for Spiritual Psychology. (My first major turning point.)
- Quit insurance job. (I was having panic attacks at work.)
- Started Insight Adventures & Coaching. (Take two.)

- Struggled for two years. (Tried to do it alone.)
- Almost quit.
- Got an awesome coach. (My second major turning point.)
- Revamped the entire way I was approaching work.
- 2012, I realized my dream!

As you can see, my life has not followed a straight-forward path. I had no special connections or opportunities handed to me. Being an entrepreneur did not come easily. Growing up, nobody around me worked for themselves. Learning to listen deeply, (a major skill of coaching) was not something that came naturally to me. Yet, the most challenging thing I had to overcome was a deep fear that I was just a dreamer in the lowest sense of the word - someone who had beautiful visions, but no long-term follow through.

After college, I bounced from job to job, quit acting, walked away from medicine and left the most lucrative job I could ever hope to have at the time. I constantly asked myself, "Who am I to start a business? Who am I to coach others about how to have a meaningful, fulfilling life?"

As a coach, I know what it feels like to live day in and day out with the constant nagging of an unrealized dream in the background. I know how it feels to be at such a low point that ending my own life felt like a viable option. I know what it feels like to be absolutely paralyzed at the precipice of a life-changing decision for months, years or even decades.

I know how it feels to know the truth and to be too scared to act on it.

That's the reason I love coaching now. I had to learn the hard way. Had it all come naturally, I wouldn't have a clue how to lead others down the path of their Wild & Precious Life.

What Do I Want to Do for the Rest of My Life?

THIS QUESTION USED TO RUN through my head almost daily, especially on the days when work was getting me down. As a coach, I hear this question, or some version of it, a lot. Though it's a very common question, it's not a very effective one to be asking yourself. It often brings up feelings of helplessness and paralysis, and rarely does it result in an answer that is useful.

Let's take a look at why this question doesn't really serve you. It presupposes that the next thing you choose to do will be the thing you do for the rest of your life. Let's be honest; the *rest of your life* is a long time, unless you're 95. Maybe that was a valid question to be asking yourself in 1950's America, but nowadays, people have many different careers in their lives and the global economy is constantly changing. Trying to predict ten, twenty or even five years down the road is next to impossible, unless you have a crystal ball (and if you have an accurate one and want to get rid of it, please send it my way!).

If you are feeling stuck and overwhelmed and ready for change, there is only one question you should be asking yourself:

"What am I going to do NEXT?"

This can be broken down into the smallest baby steps that move you forward in a direction that feels exciting to you. No business plan or 10-year future forecast needed. I find that if you look too far ahead, it's easy to get overwhelmed and not move at all.

When I led my first Insight Adventures™ retreat to Nepal, it started with me booking my plane ticket. I had no plan, no marketing, nothing - just a deep yearning and awareness that I was sick and tired of *talking* about my dream. So I took action in the simplest way I knew how. I moved in a way that I knew would get the momentum going. I had no way of knowing how it would work out. The first trip ended up being a huge success, and now I take a group every October. Will I be leading retreats to Nepal for "the rest of my life"? Who knows? For now, I do know that this is the adventure I'll be leading *next*.

Maybe you don't want to lead trips around the world. Maybe your desires are completely different. Well, this formula works for all kinds of situations...

I worked with a client who was feeling stuck and didn't know what she was going to do with the "rest of her life." We discovered that her main goal was to find a man and enter into a meaningful relationship. This was something she had wanted for years, but she just couldn't seem to work it out. And, she had a major barrier to making this happen: she worked all day in an office full of women, and each night she returned to her home in suburbia where she was surrounded by retired couples and families. She had been talking about moving to a younger area for years, but she was unable to get herself to do it. Her simple and courageous first step was to commit to the date when her home would go up for sale. This started the momentum. She sold her home within a year, moved to a young, hip area in Denver and is now in a relationship. She had no way of knowing how it would work out, but she was willing to be honest enough with herself to identify and take the next step.

For you it may be as simple as making a phone call, signing up for a retreat or committing to a simple action step that moves your forward.

So I ask you...

What one thing calls you right now? It may be a strong yearning, or just a gentle whisper.

What is the first *tiny* step you can take right now, that will move you forward?

Now. Put down this book and GO DO IT.

Send me an email at jesse@jessegros.com and share with me what you did!

Still Searching for Your Purpose?

Maturity includes the recognition that no one is going to see anything in us that we don't see in ourselves. Stop waiting for a producer. Produce yourself.
— **Marianne Williamson**

CONSIDER FOR A MOMENT that you may NEVER find your purpose. What? If that sends your energy on a nosedive or makes you feel like you want to polish off an entire pint of Ben and Jerry's and go watch three movies in a row, I understand. Don't worry. I'm an optimist and live with a very strong sense of purpose, so stay with me.

It's easy to run around caught in the cycle of, "When I find my purpose, *then* I'll take action and really move." And we go through life wishing, hoping and praying that purpose will one day hit us over the head or gently descend from the heavens. Or we take a more active role and become seekers searching for purpose, as if it's something outside of us that can be discovered, as if the missing link, the *precursor to action* is the *discovery* of our purpose. And all the while, we are waiting for permission to go out and live a meaningful life. Here's the thing, though:

You don't find your purpose; you create it.

Purpose evolves through doing. It shows itself though action, through following the hints of your desires and the subtle or not so subtle pull to be doing something different with your life. If you want a more purposeful life, the answer is to move, to take small actions in the direction you are pulled. Purpose will follow.

Don't Ask What the World Needs

Don't ask what the world needs. Ask what makes you come alive, and go do it. Because what the world needs are people who have come alive.
— Howard Thurman, African American author, philosopher, theologian, educator and civil rights leader

I KNOW I WANT TO MAKE A DIFFERENCE, but what do I do? I just love this quote by Howard Thurman because it speaks to looking at an internal frame of reference versus looking towards an external frame of reference for guidance and direction.

The world needs a lot of things. However, looking inside for what we need, or more importantly, what really lights us up, should be our highest priority. Why?

To me, coming alive is the process of aligning your thoughts, choices and actions with your inner guidance. It's attuning yourself to the message that is always there inside you, always available. One of my favorite tools for getting connected to this inner knowing comes from author and coach Martha Beck. She uses a technique called the "follow your Marmoset" response. Marmosets are these fuzzy little creatures with huge eyes. When they see something that catches their attention, their whole face pops open and their eyes bug out in the wildest way. On an inner level, humans do this all the time.

It's the response you get when you see or hear something and your whole body skips a beat. Wow! Or you get a chill that runs through your body. In that instant there is something that our inner knowing recognizes as part of our path. It says, "Hey, hey!! That's it! I want that!" All of this occurs in an instant, just before our rational mind interferes. "Oh, I could never do that. It's not logical. It's too risky. The economy is not right, etc." We have a fleeting moment of direction from our inner guidance system, and we often miss it.

That's what I'm asking you to do. Take note! Go back to the moments in your life and notice when you had this kind of response to things. Write them down. These are the crumbs on the trail that will lead you to your next steps.

Elevating the Consciousness of the Dance Floor

F OR MOST OF MY EARLY LIFE, I heard "go to college, pick a career and live a happy life in a good neighborhood, etc." However, years later, I had watched too many TED Talks to think life was just about that. How could it really just be about making a good living, buying a house and hitting the repeat button for my kids?

I wanted a real purpose, something deep, something lasting, something bigger than me. Upon reflection, I realized that I had many different mini- purposes, but many of them seemed to eventually circle back around to money and comfort. Not that these things weren't valuable, but I wanted to know that I was part of the greater picture. As my retired accountant friend put it, "You are either part of the problem or part of the solution." I wanted to know in my heart that I was part of the solution. (Recycling wasn't enough.)

Fast-forward several years to the Burning Man festival in Nevada. Riding through the desert with a group of friends, we came upon a massive open-air amphitheater called The Coliseum. The DJ was playing deep house music and hundreds of people were dancing in full costume. We joined the crowd and danced for a while until I noticed that while everyone was dancing to the music, nobody seemed to be interacting with each other. The DJ set would go all night, and I wondered if this would continue until sunrise.

As an experiment, I started to play a game I learned in graduate school. I leaned over to a woman standing next to me. "We are playing a game. Do you want to play?" I asked. She nodded yes. The music was loud. Cupping my hand over my mouth, so she could hear, I continued, "I'm going to look you in the eyes until I get a hit, and then I am going to share with you the beauty I seen in you. Then you will pass it on to a stranger, using the sentence, 'The beauty I see in you is...' And they will pass it on in turn."

"Okay!" she responded. "I have just one question. Can I play with more than one person, and can I do it outside of the arena?"

"Absolutely," I responded. I love people who think big.

Looking into her eyes, I could see a kind and compassionate woman. "The beauty I see in you is...you are a very kind and compassionate person. And sometimes maybe you give too much." Her eyes started to well up and she reached out and gave me a strong hug. "Now," I whispered in her ear, "you have one minute to pay it forward." She stopped and scanned the crowd and then looked back at me as if to say, "Do I really have to?" I pointed down to my watch and smiled back. She gathered her courage and bounced over to woman with long red hair, dancing by herself. I watched them talk and soon they too hugged and the woman with red hair danced over to a young man with a purple Mohawk to continue the game.

I watched from elevated scaffolding as the game spread for hours all over the massive arena. About halfway through, a young guy dressed in neon green fur leaned over to me. "I heard you started this thing. What are you doing?"

"I'm elevating the consciousness of the dance floor," I replied.

"You are doing what?" he asked.

"I'm elevating the consciousness of the dance floor." (Did I just say that?!) "See all of those people smiling, hugging and looking into each other's eyes? Two hours ago nobody was communicating – they were all dancing alone."

Suddenly a thought crossed my mind. *If we could do this in the arena, what if it spread beyond to the 60,000 people at Burning Man?* We danced until sunrise, until nothing but a small group remained. On our bike ride back to our camp, I didn't see thousands of people looking into each other's eyes, so it appeared that the game had not left our arena, but who really knows how many people it touched. Beyond the dance floor, it occurred to me that if it's indeed true that we are all interconnected, then what I was doing that night was elevating the consciousness of humanity - maybe on a very limited scale, for a limited time, but nevertheless it happened. I watched the smiles and the hugs. I watched people connecting with deeper levels of their humanity. I watched it travel around the arena like a love virus.

I think I permanently caught the bug, its major symptom being a newly defined sense of deep purpose:

My purpose is to elevate the consciousness of humanity. (Yes, I just said that.)

Even if it's just one person at a time.

A Special Brand of Resistance

EACH ONE OF US HAS OUR OWN special brand of resistance. It's the magic formula our ego has created to keep us safe and keep us from going outside our comfort zone. It also holds us back from realizing our destiny.

When I am working on something that really matters to me, resistance shows up disguising itself as "being reasonable." When I'm on the verge of committing to something that is meaningful and feels a bit risky, it shows up to stop me at the door on the way out.

"Being reasonable" was the very lie that had me chasing a degree in medicine. It's the voice that told me that traveling the world was nothing more than a "someday" dream. It's the voice that told me I could never charge $15,000 for a client to work with me.

How do I defend myself against the "voice of reason?" I have learned that by being unreasonable as often as possible is the counter move that keeps me moving outside of my comfort zone. I also often look back and ask myself, when has being *unreasonable* served me?

My personal short list of *unreasonable*:

It was unreasonable to think that a substitute teacher making $100 a day could in 15 months turn around and earn enough to save over $100 thousand.

It was unreasonable to think that I could quit my job in the height of the recession and in four years grow a successful coaching and retreat business.

It was very unreasonable to think that I could take vacation time during the first years of building my business. I averaged two months a year.

It was also unreasonable to think that after suffering two lung collapses, that I could years later be leading treks high in the Himalayas and Andes Mountains. (My doctors told me I would never be able to go above 10,000 feet.)

Take that, "voice of reason!"

How is *being reasonable* holding you back?

Should-ing All Over Yourself

HOW MUCH TIME HAS BEEN WASTED in the world by very capable people indulging in the thought that things *should* be different? How many millions of productive hours are wasted in this thought every day, instead of being focused on a solution?

The biggest challenge with *should-ing* all over yourself, besides the fact that it stinks, is that it's based on a fundamental lie. To believe that anything *should* be different is to argue with reality. It's like saying that the sun *should* not be coming up so early. Or the moon *should* not be so bright tonight.

I wasted a lot of energy early on focused on the thought: *I should be further along in my life right now.* By believing this thought, I created a lot of unnecessary pain for myself. Byron Katie would ask, "Is that true? Is it really true that this fact of life presenting itself in this moment is somehow false, simply because you are upset about it?" Trapped in upset, I was not only buying into a false belief, but I was also giving up my ability to be present and ended up missing out on many of the opportunities and solutions that were passing right in front of me.

A client of mine, Tom, was working on a large funding proposal for tens of millions of dollars. He was extremely stressed and felt like things were starting to spiral out of his control. Coming from a corporate background, Tom was used to working on a tight, highly organized schedule. In contrast, his business partner James, a prolific freelance writer, had worked on a very loose and free flowing schedule for most of his adult life. Deadline after deadline was pushed out and things were coming to a head.

Tom's major complaint was this: "James *should* get things done on time and be more organized (like me)!"

I asked him, "Is that true? Is it *really true* that James *should* get things done on time and be organized (like you)"?

"Yes! He should!" he barked.

"Why is that, Tom?" I asked gently.

"Because that's how business is done! That's how you *should* be if you want to succeed!"

He was really digging into his position. I inquired further. "James is extremely successful at what he does, using his *formula*, right? Is it possible that there is more than one way to succeed?" There was a long pause.

"Yeah, but he drives me crazy!"

"Ah okay, that's different," I responded. "Is there any realistic chance that you are going to get him to change?" I asked.

"No. He's basically set in his ways. He can really do whatever he wants." Tom started to calm down.

"So is it fair to say that you have two very different, but equally *effective* styles of getting things done? And indeed he is very organized, in his very go-with-the-flow, unique, James kind of way?" There was another long pause.

"Ok...sure," he agreed, sounding a bit defeated.

"Tom, I want you to try this on, just to see how it feels. "James *should not* get things done on time." He laughed out loud. "Your turn," I prodded.

"James should *not* get things done on time?" he said, confused.

"Say it again."

"James should not get things done on time." This time it sounded like a statement.

"One more time," I said.

"James should not get things done on time!" This time, it rung so true that we both started laughing. I joined in.

"James should *definitely not* get things done on time! Ha!" Tom responded, getting really excited.

"Seriously...whatever he does, James should definitely not get things in on time!" More laughter. That was the last time we ever spoke about James *needing to be different* than he was.

Tom shared with me the other day that he has created a solution to his "should-ing" problem! On his desk, he has a stack of index cards with his "shoulds" written on one side of the card and the truths written on the other side. Anytime he's feeling upset and demanding that something should be different than it is, he pulls out that card and flips it over to remind himself of the truth. Immediately he stops fighting reality, usually lets out a huge laugh and gets back to work.

Is there any way you are "should-ing" on yourself and keeping yourself from moving forward in your life?

Get Off My Porch!

You don't have to believe everything you think.
— **Bumper sticker**

WHAT STORY HAVE YOU MADE UP that *feels real, feels true,* that is keeping you from what you want?

During a powerful scene in the movie *Fight Club*, Tyler Durden, the lead character, is in the process of recruiting members for his underground movement. The word has gotten out and young men are starting to show up on the front porch of his rundown house, waiting for a chance to join the movement. They are exhausted, bored and disillusioned by their everyday lives. These men are searching for meaning, purpose and the chance to be a part of something bigger than themselves. (Not unlike many young and middle-aged people today.)

Tyler devises a scheme to deal with the people on the doorstep. Tyler says, "If the applicant is young, we tell him he's too young. Old, too old. Fat, too fat." From then on, anyone who shows up is insulted and made to stand outside. Tyler instructs "Only if the applicant waits at the door for three days without food, shelter or encouragement, can he enter the building and begin training."

While this may sound overly harsh, is it any different than what we do to ourselves? If anything, it's easier and more kind than the level of abuse we are capable of putting ourselves through. Looking back at the past five years, if you had given me the choice of standing out in the cold for three days without food rather than face my own doubts, fears and insecurities, I would have chosen Tyler's doorstep any day.

How many years have you been holding onto your story? The story that has you out in the cold, waiting for your life to begin?

I'll share with you the story that kept me standing out on the porch of my own life for years.

It went something like this: I am smart, I know this. I am capable, I know this. I even know deep down in my heart what I want to do, if I'm willing to admit it to myself. But, I need to make money. I have to choose something reliable. I can't just follow my heart. That feels totally irresponsible. What if I don't make it and all of my friends have passed me by and gone on to be successful and I am still struggling? I have to choose something predictable. I don't want to end up homeless out on the street. So I'll just choose something really safe and then after I have made my money, *then* I'll go after what I really want. Besides, nobody listens to people unless they are financially successful. You can't follow your heart and make it in this world unless you are very rich, connected or very, very lucky.

I told myself some version of this story for over 15 years.

Out on the porch, I would have yelled at myself:

"Jesse, you're too inexperienced! You have never run a business! You're too attached to quick financial success! AND...*you are just too damn scared to try!*"

Out on the porch...what stops you?

I'm too_____

I'm too_____

I'm too_____

Fill this list out exhaustively, and get clear about your story. Get very specific about the reasons you tell yourself you can't have what you want.

I bet not one of them is *really true.*

There is No "There" —
Enter the Purposeful Life

These days man knows the price of everything,
but the value of nothing.
— **Oscar Wilde**

THROUGHOUT MY EARLY TO MID-THIRTIES I constantly had this feeling that someday, I would "get my life together." And once I got it together, life would be grand. I was painfully aware that there was more that I wanted out of life and just around the corner was "there," that mystical place where we arrive and suddenly feel complete.

When I bought my first car in high school, I discovered that there was no "there," a discovery that I soon forgot. For years I had dreamed about how my life would radically change when I got some wheels. I imagined friends all riding with me at lunch, driving to parties and people hanging out around my car at school. After working and saving for several years, I bought my first car at 17 years old. I felt so free. Within less than a month, though, I felt a huge letdown inside. This thing I had dreamed of and all that went with it, soon felt like just another part of my life - nothing special. I didn't feel like a different person as I had imagined I would. Damn!

This was my first experience with the hedonic treadmill. The hedonic treadmill is the tendency of humans to quickly re-

31

turn to a relatively stable level of happiness despite major positive or negative events. In the case of buying new things, we usually get a purchaser's high, which inevitably fades, as the "newness" wears off and it's back to normal. In essence, no matter where we live, what we drive or what our finances are, there is no way around this simple human tendency. No car, home, new toy or clothing will be "the" thing that gets us "there." How disappointing to realize that so much of what we are told through media and advertising just sets us up to lose. It sets us up to forever want more. It sets us up to devote our lives to the least satisfying and basically meaningless pursuit of material items.

I have heard so many clients and friends over time say things like, "Once I get this much in my savings" or "Once I have the house, or a second house, then I'll be complete and I can relax and really enjoy life."

I'm not saying don't have nice things; I'm just aware that shiny new things always become just regular things in time. There is no *thing* in this world that will give us what we are truly seeking.

Just ask the men who walked on the moon about the emotional staying power of getting "there."

There is no "there."

Enter: the purposeful life.

COURAGE

Deep in our hearts we know what we are here to do in this life-time. Whether we choose to admit it to ourselves or keep it locked away is a matter of courage. For once our deep desires are made known to ourselves and others, the magnetic pull will never leave us alone. And this bold act cannot be reversed.

We may attempt to run, hide or numb ourselves from our truth, but eventually we must act.

These are stories about people I know and have worked with, who have summoned their courage to follow their inner guidance and reap great rewards.

And the day came when the risk to remain tight in a bud was more painful than the risk it took to blossom.
— Anais Nin

I Want to Be a
National Geographic Photographer

I T STARTED LIKE THIS: "I am done with my job!" Jill was working for a real estate firm in San Francisco, showing homes and doing office work. "Every day, I dread going to work."

"Jill, I have a question for you. Now this may seem trite or even overly optimistic, but I'm going to ask you anyway. If you could do anything...what would you do?"

Without hesitation, she responded: "I would be a National Geographic photographer." Her answer was so clear and direct, it hit me right in the chest.

"Well then. That's what you have to do," I said. Then I waited for her to divulge all of her fears and rationalizations about why this was too big of a leap. It didn't happen. In less than a year, Jill was on a plane to Southeast Asia with a camera in hand. No experience, no inside connections, just a vision.

Five years later, Jill found herself in a large room in Washington D.C. The room was full of seasoned photographers and journalists. Looking around, she was by far the youngest person in the room. It was full of people she had once looked up to, and could now call her colleagues: a room full of National Geographic photographers just like her.

Meet Shannon Galpin

The world tries to break everyone and some people are stronger in the places that were broken.
— **Ernest Hemingway**

I MET SHANNON GALPIN at the Telluride Mountain Film Festival. She is an adventurer, an athlete, an activist and a mother. She was giving a talk about her non-profit Mountain2Mountain, where she is working with young women in Afghanistan to empower them and break generations of oppression.

Midway through her talk about her courageous work, she shared something with a silent and captivated audience. "People always ask me, what was it that inspired me to make such a radical change in life? What inspired me to leave my profession, sell my home and step into the work I am doing today? I have never shared this with a live audience before..." she said.

There was a long pause and she began. "Many years ago, when I was walking home from work, I was brutally attacked, raped and left for dead...a victim at 18. I did not share my experience with many people, as I was petrified of being labeled a *victim*. But it wasn't until 13 years later when the same violence struck my only sister that I decided to do something about it...

"I thought about my young daughter. *How could I look her in the face and explain that in my lifetime, I did nothing about this?* At the time, Afghanistan was ranked as the world's worst place for women. So I decided I would start there. In that moment, I made my decision to risk everything to create a world that was just...where women who are victimized are not destined to be victims, bound by circumstances out of their control. If they had a voice, they could be solutions."

When she chose to leave her comfortable life behind to make a difference, Shannon had a lot at stake, not just for herself but also for her daughter who she was raising as a single mom. She received a lot of criticism from other mothers about the dangerous nature of her work and her decision to sell her home.

Her courage and action has paid off and Mountain2Mountain has grown into a formidable voice for women. She was recently interviewed by *The New York Times* and was voted as one of National Geographic's Adventurers of the Year for her humanitarian efforts. Her work in Afghanistan is giving young women all over the world hope that change is possible, even in a place as challenging as Afghanistan. You can see what she is up to at:

www.mountain2mountain.org.

Madeline —
The Wedding Is Already Set

ADELINE WAS 25 YEARS OLD when her best friend came to me. "You really need to help her out, Jesse. She's rushing into a marriage that I really don't think is going to work. She's having tremendous second thoughts about it, but she feels trapped. The wedding has already been paid for, the guest list has been sent out. She feels totally trapped."

"Well, does she have a sense of what she really wants?" I asked.

"Yeah, she wants to travel the world."

Two days later I met Madeline at an Italian restaurant to talk about her situation. She shared that she really loved her fiancé Dan, but she had some huge reservations about getting married and had a tremendous dream to travel, one that her soon-to-be husband did not share. I pulled out some travel albums of mine and her eyes started to tear up.

"I really just don't know what to do. I feel so horrible. I feel like I would be letting everyone else down."

"Well... it sounds to me like if you don't follow your heart, you will be letting yourself down in a tremendous way," I told her. "If you don't follow your heart on this, you are not only lying to yourself, but you are also lying to your fiancé about your true desires. If you choose to just suck it up, this will most likely foster deep resentment."

If you love someone, let them go. If they return to you,
it was meant to be. If they don't, their love was never yours to
begin with...
— **Unknown**

After our meeting, she agreed that this is what she had to do. Several months later she broke off the engagement, quit her job and got on a plane to Central America for what would become a 10-month adventure of self-discovery.

Distanced from all of the peer pressure of her family and fiancé, it quickly became very clear to Madeline that Dan was not the man for her.

Three years after her travels, she married a different man, and now lives in the Bay Area with her husband and their two children. The last time we spoke, she said that she was very happy and could not wait for her children to be old enough to travel.

Follow Your Bliss Like Brian Johnson

WHAT IF I FEEL LIKE I'M NOT CLEAR about what to do next? But I'm damn sure it's not what I'm doing right now?

I feel like, if I had clarity about the next chapter of my life, I could make the move into something new.

The answer to this dilemma lies not in waiting for clarity, but in taking action. You cannot have clarity without action. You have not earned the right to a closer view of your future until you get out on the street, take risks and act. It's in the "doing" that clarity evolves piece by piece.

It's very rare that people have a complete future vision of their lives and live it out.

So you might be asking, "But what do I do when I don't know the next steps to take? You do what the great American philosopher Joseph Campbell suggests. You:

Follow your bliss.

One of my favorite examples of someone following their bliss out of misery and into success comes from Brian Johnson, the creator of Philosopher's Notes. He shares the story of how he left law school after his first year and moved back home with his mother. He also ended a five-year relationship in the same week! He shared that his head was spinning for months and that he found himself at such a low point, he entertained various ways of ending it all. He knew he had to leave law, but had no clue where to go next. The *only thing* he wanted to do was to coach Little League baseball. In his hour of darkness, the only light he could see was a tiny little glimmer coming from a volunteer position in children's sports - not exactly what you would call a glorious next step after law school!

He moved on it and become a very mediocre t-ball coach, living at home. Months later, he got the idea of creating an online network linking parents, coaches and players. This little project turned into a thriving company called E-Teams, which Brian sold in a couple of years and was replaced by the CEO of Adidas! Since then he has built several businesses, traveled the world and married the love of his life.

All of this came from Brian following his bliss in his darkest hour, even though in the big picture it really didn't make any sense. He did not have clarity or a divine download from God telling him his purpose. All he had was a small clue leading him toward great things that were waiting for him just around the corner.

David Rollins

DAVID ROLLINS IS SOMEONE I HIGHLY RESPECT. He's a visionary with a heart and a crystal clear conscience. He's my friend and has also been a client. Early in his medical career, he walked away from his medical residency. He left based on a deep conviction that he did not believe in the direction his field was headed. It was a bold move, considering how much work it took him to get to that point in his life.

Later he worked for one of the premier consulting companies in the country. He was one of the few people who mathematically predicted the 2008 housing crash. His findings were ignored by his clients who were already making too much money to take his warnings seriously. Again he left a lucrative position out of personal precedent and entered a different industry.

He then turned his energy toward long distance running. This is when I met David. On the drive home after successfully completing a long endurance race, he shared with me a dream about revolutionizing the way America thinks about health care and obesity. It was an idea that he had been sitting on for a long time. And for good reason. His vision for a national non-profit would directly challenge the established beliefs of the American medical institution and likely be an uphill battle for the next ten to fifteen years. He would also have to leave his steady paycheck and take a huge pay cut. With his family and hefty mortgage to consider, this was no small matter.

When we started working together, David was an extremely accomplished man by any standard, was riddled with insecurity and worried about the sanity of ditching the American dream (his current life) to "save the world." He was all too aware of the personal sacrifices he would have to make for the greater good.

"It's people like you who change the world." I shared.

"What if I fail? What will my son think about me?" He asked.

"Your son will know that his father bravely gave up comfort and security for a chance to make a huge impact in millions of people's lives. You are leading the way, not just for you and your cause, but for everyone around you."

David agreed that is was a risk worth taking. And with a tremendous amount of courage and great personal risk, David walked away from his steady paycheck to start his non-profit. Along with his partner, he raised $5,000,000 in initial startup money his first year! His non-profit is up and running at full speed and already making waves in the medical community. All of his initial paralyzing worries and doubts never materialized.

I am in awe of the magnitude of the venture David has begun, and I am thankful for having the opportunity to support him through the creation phase of his potentially game changing mission.

It is often when our doubts and fears are screaming STOP! That success is waiting just one step away.
— **Dr. Logan**

Honey...I Think I Want to Be a Lion Tamer

"**D**O YOU THINK YOU COULD DRIVE ME to a job interview, Pete? My car is in the shop."

This was the beginning of a life-changing moment for my father. That morning, he drove his friend to a job interview and waited in the lobby. The interview was for a unique position as an apprentice lion tamer for a small animal park in Northern California. After waiting for a while, a voice came into the room. "Next." The woman gestured for my father to go in. He wasn't there for an interview. He already had his career lined up. The week before, he had just been hired on with an insurance agency for what looked to be the beginning of a long, promising career in sales. He had a company car and an expense account and was heading in for his welcome party the next day.

On a whim, he went into the interview. "Just for fun," he thought. He was so relaxed and had a great time with the interviewer. The next day, they called him. "Peter, we want you." He lit up with energy, and in a moment, that was it, he knew this is what he wanted to do with his life. He called my mother. "Honey, I want to be a lion tamer. I don't want to sell insurance." There was a short pause.

"If this is what you want to do, I'll support you and it looks like I'm going back to work," my mother replied. He called the insurance group, explained what had happened and in that moment his whole life trajectory changed.

He worked in a wild animal park for 25 years, eventually was hired on as co-host for Mutual of Omaha's Wild Kingdom television show and to this day continues to travel the country educating young people and sharing his message of hope and conservation. He loves to share this story about how he landed what he considers to be the "best job on the planet."

Had he ignored his feelings and just passed them off as a fantasy, life would have looked very different.

Old Folks Home Escapee
Patrice Williams

It is not true that people stop pursuing dreams because
they grow old, they grow old because they stop
pursuing dreams.
— **Gabriel Garcia Marquez**

I MET 69-YEAR-OLD PATRICE WILLIAMS while canyoneering with friends at the Vermilion Cliffs National Monument in Arizona. We were at the information center, getting the details on a slot canyon we were very excited to explore. Eying us thoroughly, she shared:

"I wouldn't go down in those canyons if I were you, boys. Even though it's sunny here, there are thunderstorms dumping rain in the mountains nearby. That water can make its way down here pretty quickly and hit you with a flash flood. Once you get down in those slot canyons, that wall of water can be over 10 feet tall. If that hits you, you're a goner. And, once you're down in there, there is no easy way out. Now, that said...you do what you want."

I really didn't have a good feeling about it. Having been almost caught in a flash flood before, I didn't want to take any risks. My canyoneering partners were not as cautious and were ready to go out and see what the weather was doing. It was very hard to judge, since where we were it was sunny and there were almost no clouds in sight.

In at attempt to stall and give us more time to get information about what we were getting into, I started warming up to Patrice. She was clearly in the later years of her life, but was full of energy and spunk. "Tell me, how did you get here?" I asked.

"Well that's a long story, Jesse."

"I have time," I said, again wanting to stall a bit.

"Four years ago, my kids put me in an old folks home. I lasted about two weeks and decided I needed to get the hell out of there! So I devised an escape plan and one morning I slipped out, 'stole' my car, went to an outfitting store, got some back-packing gear, some food and a map and took off to do the Appalachian Trail with my dog Lucy. By the end of that day I was on the trail. I didn't leave a note for my family because I wanted to get far enough on the trail so they couldn't come get me. I figured it would be a good couple of days until rangers found my car at the trailhead and by then I would be far enough along that they would have to wait 10 days or so until I reached the first town.

"On the trail I met all kinds of really nice young people and they really helped me out. Even though I wasn't the fastest walker, some of them would walk with me for a day or two and then take off. Then another would catch up to me and talk for while. I was rarely alone for more than a day. It was great. They couldn't believe I was out here at 65, alone with my dog. I told them I was an escaped convict from the old folks home for the dying.

"Once I reached the next town, where you can go for supplies, all my kids were there, waiting for me, worried, upset and hell-bent on getting me to return to that God-awful home for drugged-up zombies. And the best thing was, they got to meet a bunch of the young people who were now in town, getting supplies. They vouched for me and shared about how great I was doing on the trail. I put up a real fight with my kids. I told them I would rather get eaten by a bear on the trail here than go back.

"After spending the whole day together, they finally gave up and decided that they would each take turns bringing me supplies at the food drop points and towns that the trail goes through. Well, I would always ask for much more than I needed, so I could help out these young people on the trail. They all had one thing in common...lots of time and no money. So I asked for beef jerky and M&Ms and all kinds of good stuff.

"After about two months, I was done and my little Lucy was definitely done. I finished up the trail and my kids all came to meet me. My son suggested that I apply to work for the National Park Service. I got the job after a couple of months, and well, here I am. Been doing this for a bit over three years. About every six to eight months I get a new assignment in a new location. I just love it! My kids bought me a little airstream trailer and a truck to pull it. It's right out there in the back. That's it. My husband has been gone for years. My kids all have their lives and I have mine. I'm the happiest I have ever been. And you know...I just love people and I get to meet all kinds of nice folks from all over the world. Lots of Europeans travel in the national parks, you know. So there you are, that's my story...and I still think you all should reconsider going down in those canyons."

Listening to Patrice, I had a smile from ear to ear. She had just single-handedly given me hope for my later years in life. I had been feeling trapped by the old model of working for the first two-thirds of my life just so I could then be comfortable in the last third, which now seemed like such a rip-off. I never understood the concept of retirement anyway. If I found myself at

69 years old working at a national park, that would be awesome!

Unable to detour my friends, we headed off to go find the slot canyon. For hours we walked through the desert on simple trails. Dingo, my fearless cancer-surviving Australian friend, chose to walk in the bottom of a dry river bed, the exact place a flash flood would roll through. We walked a bit further, and then we heard it – a deep rumble. I knew immediately it could only be one thing. "Flash flood!" I yelled and went running full speed, leaping over cacti, rocks and bushes yelling "flood, flood, flood!" I reached the riverbank just in time to see a 5-foot tall wall of mud, tree branches and debris come speeding around the corner. Dingo had heard the rumble and climbed up the steep bank just in time. When we arrived, he was standing at the edge of the river flashing us his "I know what I'm doing" smile. He always knew what he was doing.

"Cheeky bastard!" I yelled, smiling. Looked like we were going back to the ranger station for another round of stories!

Deposit Slips to Scuba Tanks

"I HATE MY JOB! Ugh, I hate my job!" This was my brother John's morning ritual before donning his suit, tie and leather shoes to head off to the bank for another day of corporate drudgery.

I, on the other hand, enjoyed a very flexible schedule teaching sports to autistic children. Most of my days were spent outdoors rock climbing, hiking, biking and surfing. My brother, on the other hand, was stuck in an office and miserable. It didn't help him to watch me heading off to "work" every day in surf trunks.

One day I just said to him, "Why don't you quit! You have some savings; leave your job and do what you have been talking about for years - go be a scuba diving instructor."

He resisted. "Yeah but..."

"Yeah, but what?" I replied. "How big is your *yeah butt* getting?!"

This conversation went on for months, until one day he declared that he was going to do it! Strolling into his office, with the air of the guy from the movie *Office Space*, he explained to his boss that, well... yeah...he would be needing Wednesdays off from now on. He would be happy to come in on Saturdays instead. His boss looked at him with utter confusion. "Why is that, John?"

"Well...you see...I have signed up for a scuba instructor class on Wednesdays. It was the only one available this fall."

"Okay...?" she stammered in disbelief.

"Once I have my instructor's license, I'm quitting this job and am going to travel the world as a freelance scuba instructor." He smiled.

"You can't do that...I mean, I can't authorize that." She responded quickly.

With newfound confidence John butted in, "Go ask Steven, the manager. Go ask him." She stomped off and minutes later returned with a flushed face.

"The answer is no, John." John laughed. "Oh...sorry to hear that. Well then, I quit."

Four months later, John boarded a plane for what turned into a 2½ year trip around the world working as a freelance scuba instructor. "He must have had connections or something," you might think. No, he just showed up in Bali, rented a scooter for $3 a day, purchased a local cell phone for $20 and printed 100 business cards. Several weeks later, he was working part-time as an instructor and in a month he had a full schedule working part-time for several companies on call. All the while, he never signed a contract and kept his schedule completely under his control.

His work took him around the globe to the world's greatest diving spots in Bali, Thailand and the Seychelles - to name a few. From a burned-out, out of shape, angry banker to a lean, healthy reader of Buddhist philosophy, his whole world changed because he had the courage to leave the safety of his 9 to 5.

Interestingly enough, after John quit his job, the corporate headquarters called him and asked him what they would need to do in order to get him to come back. "There is nothing you could offer me that would make me come back," he responded.

John has since returned from his adventure around the world and is now pursuing a career as a firefighter.

Surfing Your Way to a Ph.D.

*Deep play is that more intensified form of play
that puts us in a rapturous mood and awakens the most
creative, sentient, and joyful aspects of our inner selves.*
— **Diane Ackerman, author, poet, essayist,
and naturalist**

TOM G. IS A PH.D. RESEARCH SCIENTIST and is also an avid surfer. He shared that, while many people in his graduate school lab were putting in 12-hour days, trying to force ideas and solutions, he was rarely at work for more than six hours a day. The rest of the time he was surfing, playing video games or sleeping.

Surely this wasn't the behavior of a dedicated scientist? And yet, often when we were out in the water, sitting in the line-up waiting for the next set to roll through, Tom would turn to me and say, "I just figured it out!" He would start explaining some complex theory to me and I would listen intently pretending to understand. "All of my best ideas, including my dissertation came while I was surfing," he says. Even now that he is out of school and work life has become more demanding, he still makes time to surf every day, not only for the fun of it, but as a vital part of his creative process.

For adults, it's easy to forget how to play and even easier to dismiss it as not important. When are you in deep play? Maybe it's been a while. You may even have to look back to your earlier years to find it. Whatever it is, go do it. Do a lot of it and your work life will thrive.

Davia King — Artist & Budding World Traveler

FROM AN EMAIL I SENT OUT to my mailing list:

Hi family!

I have a fun and inspiring story to share with you.

Two months ago, I received a phone call from artist Davia King. She shared with me that it was one of her life dreams to travel to Peru with me in May. And, she said, "I'm not sure how I can afford to go on your trip."

There was a brief pause.

"Great!" I responded. "That's one of my favorite things to hear!"

Again there was a pause on the phone; my answer hadn't been what she had expected. You see, I love working with people about getting creative about money.

"What do you do?" I asked.

"I work at a hotel and I'm an artist," she shared.

"Have you ever sold your art?" I asked.

She had, but only a couple times. I shared with her, "If you commit to Peru, I will help you raise funds to go on the trip."

It took her about two seconds to decide. "I'm in!"

Within two hours she had purchased her plane ticket and the adventure began. We hosted two art events with Davia, and I'm happy to share that she paid for her whole trip by SELLING HER ART - in less than six weeks!

Done!

It takes a lot of courage to put yourself out there, and Davia did it in a big way.

SO, I ask you...what big experience have you put off because you DIDN'T HAVE THE MONEY?

Maybe it's not the money that's in the way...

How creative and courageous are you willing to be to have the experiences you deeply desire?

An additional note: During our trip to Peru, Davia sold another large piece of her art to one of the other participants on the trip. She not only paid for her trip, but actually made a profit, just by committing to the adventure. She now has her eyes on some much bigger goals in Hollywood, goals that she never before would have allowed herself to dream.

Howie

I FIRST MET HOWARD, or Howie as he likes to be called, in June of 2009. At 6AM in the morning, out in front of my home in San Diego, Howie, his son Lee and my friend Deanna were all loading their gear into my Toyota® 4Runner. It was the morning of my inaugural Insight Adventures™ trip!

At the time, Howie was 76 years old and had recently been written up in the newspaper for his unique, active lifestyle.

The article read:

"Howard Schwartz, 76, pedals his kayak home, after paddling six hours from the Catamaran Hotel out to the ocean and back. Six days a week, Schwartz wakes up before dawn, dives into his pool to get his blood flowing and bicycles from his home in North Pacific Beach to the Catamaran for his six-hour bay-to-ocean journey. A retired house painter of 24 years, Schwarz has lived in Pacific Beach for 25 years. Six years ago, Schwartz sold his truck and began transporting his kayak via bicycle. 'The gas prices were getting too high,' he said."

Now it was time for Howie to take his kayak skills and apply them on a real expedition. After a grueling 10-hour drive down the curvy, two-lane Baja 1, we arrived at our destination on the Sea of Cortez. The next morning, we paddled several miles offshore with fully-loaded expedition kayaks. Howie paddled strong the whole way out. I was so impressed.

Each day we left our camp on Coronado Island and paddled to a new destination. We swam, hiked and spearfished. Some days the temperatures reached the high 90's and there was very little shade. It was a true hard-core adventure.

On the 4th day I asked him, "Howie, what's your secret? How are you so healthy and active?" Howie explained: I eat the same simple food every day. I paddle my kayak six days a week. Every day I take the bus to visit my girlfriend and we watch movies. And my life is good. And you know... he shared, "I have not been to a doctor in twenty years and I don't intend to visit any time soon!" Amazed, I looked over at his son, Lee.

"It's true man, he hasn't."

I felt like I had just met a man from an entirely different generation. Howie has forever altered my image of what is possible in old age.

Two years later, at 78 years old, I saw him at a Mexican restaurant. He grabbed my shoulder, pulled me aside and he said, "Whenever you are ready to go back, I'm in!"

What if Only One Person Shows Up?

S TANDING ON A WOODEN DOCK overlooking Lake Tahoe on a crisp, winter day, I was on the phone speaking with a client. The view was amazing: glassy emerald water, snowcapped mountains in the background, snow-covered beaches and the warm sun on my skin. I was struck by the serenity and sheer raw beauty of the moment. On the line was a woman feeling scared and nervous about leading her first paid workshop.

"What if nobody shows up?" she asked.

"Then you can pack up, go out to dinner and nobody will know...you won't have any witnesses!" I joked, trying to calm her nerves. "You know, what you should really be thinking about is what if only one person shows up? Would you still lead it?"

I shared with her this story: I have a very good friend, Lacy, who was starting out her career as a therapist. She and her partner had put a lot of energy and heart into creating what they felt would be an amazing two-day workshop at a local university. They advertised in as many different places they could think of and shared their event with family and friends. Many people expressed interest in their event.

On the day of the workshop, they stood behind the main stage curtain of a large room lined with chairs ready to accommodate a group of people. Thirty minutes before the event started, the room was empty. Ten minutes before the event, the room was still empty. Finally, a lone woman showed up and sat down.

The clock now read five minutes past the start time and there was only one person in the audience. One! Lacy was so upset and ashamed she told her partner that she wanted to cancel the event. Her partner held firm and they decided to lead the event and give the woman who showed up the best that they could offer! For the rest of the day, the three of them went through the workshop. What a lucky woman – she had two trained instructors all to herself!

On the second day, a woman was passing by and inquired about the event. "Join us!" Lacy said. And she did. The four of them had a deeply moving experience and were grateful the event hadn't been canceled. Days later, Lacy received a message from the second woman. She worked for the university where the event had been held and offered Lacy a job to lead workshops and a class on campus! Lacy had landed a stable, well-paying job doing the thing she loved best, all because she wasn't afraid to take a risk and lead a workshop for one.

CONSCIOUS CREATION

Adventures in Building a Conscious Business in the Heart of a Recession

Conscious Creation is about slowing down, getting quiet and creating space for your natural wisdom to guide you. It's about connecting to your deepest motivations and taking action in ways that empower you to be the greatest expression of who you really are.

When I walked away from my career in late 2008, I knew that I would not be able to build my business using my old work mantras of competitiveness, scarcity and every man for himself. I knew that I would have to redefine not only how I thought about business, but also how I showed up in my personal and professional life.

What I learned during this four-year period comprise some of the core teachings I use when working with clients who want to expand their businesses or start a new one.

Get Your Relationship With Money Straight

A VERY POWERFUL RELATIONSHIP that's worth looking at is your relationship to money. We think about it a lot and we do all kinds of strange things to acquire more of it. Most of us are totally unaware that we have a specific relationship to money, just like we have a relationship with a friend or loved one.

And just like in a relationship with a person, there is always room for improvement. Discovering and healing my conflicting thoughts and emotions around money was a huge step in the growth of my coaching and retreat business.

Discovering my false beliefs about money:

False thought #1: Money is hard to get and I will have to suffer to get it.

I discovered this in a life-coaching session with a mentor of mine. She walked me through a visualization process that I now teach to my clients. She asked me to close my eyes and visualize money. I imagined a steep cliff and on top of it there it was, locked in a big gold chest, guarded from others. I would have to scale the sandy cliffs to get to the top, where the money lived. It felt like a lot of work and not much fun.

She asked me what I would rather be doing instead of climbing that steep cliff. What I really wanted to be doing was to help people down in the village, not be alone scaling the mountain. "What if the money just flowed down the river and while you were helping the people, you could just dip in and grab some as needed?" she asked.

"I would love that!" I responded. Especially since for me, money was always a means, never the ultimate goal. A new thought occurred to me. *What if money was there to support my greatest passions rather than to keep me away from them?* This subtle shift in consciousness was the beginning of my journey into redefining my relationship with money.

False thought #2: Money will corrupt the purity of my work.

When I started my coaching practice, I ran into a common block I hear artists, healers and coaches talk about – the misunderstanding that money will somehow corrupt the purity of their work, as if there is more honesty in work done from a place of poverty. I feel quite the opposite.

I don't think money corrupts; I think people with bad relationships with money corrupt their own experiences.

Clients sometimes say to me, "I don't know how to charge for my services. I get uncomfortable. I wish I didn't have to think about money; I just want to help people."

Money as Service

Early on, I found myself wishing for the same thing. I was faced with a dilemma: how could I reconcile my conflicting desire to grow my business and make more money with my desire to help and serve people? At the time, I thought they were mutually exclusive. I had this belief that high earners got there by being cutthroats and by manipulating people, a belief solidified by an early job I had working in a shady part of the financial services industry.

With the help of my coach, I was able to see that everything I was up to in the world was based on serving others. I wasn't out in the world trying to deceive people into giving away their money or spending it in a way that was wasteful or harmful. The more I helped and the more I served, the more money I received. I also refused to engage with any business or client that didn't feel 100 percent honest or "clean."

Money as Exchange

David Elliott, a Los Angeles based healer, taught me an even easier way to relate to money. I learned that on an even deeper level, when it comes to money and providing services for people, all we are really doing is exchanging energy. For example, a client of mine puts energy into writing a legal contract, and she gets paid for her time and effort. She in turn exchanges money with me for my services of time and effort. In this case, money is nothing more than a placeholder of energy. The money I receive from her for my services is just an exchange.

Once I was able to see my work as service and money as exchange, all of my negative associations with money started to fade. Money ceased to be a thing. There is no such thing as a "real" value of an item or service; it's all made up. Something is only worth what someone is willing to pay for it. The only value is in the exchange.

Still with me? Okay. So how did this show up in the "real world?" I continued to grow my business and most importantly, the tight grip I used to have around money all but disappeared, allowing me to not only make more money, but also to give more to the charities , people and causes I believe in.

Recently, I ran into an old acquaintance at a coffee shop. He was having a really rough time with his business and was living out of a storage container. He shared that he didn't have a place to stay that night. It was already dark, so I bought him a hotel room for the night, something I would have never felt free to do in the past. In this case, abundance did not corrupt me, as I had once feared, but rather, it opened me up to being a more giving and sharing person.

But I Don't Have the Money...
Is That True?

THE MOST COMMON REASON I hear from people about why they are not doing something they deeply desire to do, is: "I don't have the money." As if to say, "not having the money" is a valid reason to not be truly living their lives. "No, you don't understand, I really don't have the money," they insist.

And I respond, "I hear you. However, I hear something different. I hear that you are looking at it as a barrier, rather than as a challenge that can be solved. Or you have just not *yet* engaged in a creative process to see how you can solve it. Or maybe this thing you say you want isn't worth stretching out of your comfort zone to *find the money* to make it happen.

At 25 years old, I found myself in this very place. I had a dream to travel the world, but I "didn't have the money." And boy did it feel true! And I would have been happy to show you my account balance of zero! More importantly, I hadn't made traveling the world an absolute necessity, something so important that I would hold a deep place of regret in my heart if I never did it. It was to be forever on my "someday" list.

Until one is committed, there is hesitancy, the chance to draw back, always ineffectiveness. Concerning all acts of initiative (and creation), there is one elementary truth, the ignorance of which kills countless ideas and splendid plans: that

the moment one definitely commits oneself, then providence moves too. *A whole stream of events issues from the decision, raising in one's favor all manner of unforeseen incidents, meetings and material assistance, which no man could have dreamt would have come his way.*
—**W.H. Murray, Scottish explorer**

This is the story of how I overcame my story of "not having enough money" at 25 years old.

Step 1: Commit

"Dad...I'm going to raise fifteen thousand dollars to travel around the world!" That's how it all started, with a phone call. Five months after September 11th, 2001, my 25-year-old sense of invulnerability had been shaken to its core. Someday became today and putting off my dream was no longer an option. I would be stepping onto a plane on Sept 11th, 2002!

Step 2: Share Your Dream

I told everyone about my grand scheme. "I'm quitting my job and taking off to travel the world!" The key part of this plan was that in the beginning there was NO PLAN, only a deep commitment to raise the needed funds. I really had no way of knowing how I would do it. I had an empty bank account and had not been able to save a penny up to that point in my life.

Step 3: Make It a Game

Before I started, I got some great advice. "Take that $15,000 and break it down into tiny pieces." Divided over nine months, it came to be $56 a day! Now THAT sounded doable! My story of needing to raise thousands of dollars changed to, "I am saving $56 a day to travel the world!" Ways to cut costs and extra opportunities to make money started popping up everywhere!

People at work gave me their shifts and I stopped buying four-dollar coffees at Starbucks. Raising the money became a fun game.

Step 4: Cut Off Exit Strategies

Eight weeks after my decision, I was flying high, riding the wave of momentum, until I hit a roadblock. I looked at my finances and I was $1000 behind schedule! Fear crept in and I started to wonder if I was dreaming too big. In that moment, I realized I had to change my approach. I gathered my courage, walked into work and asked my boss for a twenty percent raise to help fund my trip. "Oh and by the way, I will be quitting in seven months," I shared. My hands were shaking. I held my breath and smiled. She agreed! Now my boss would be looking for my replacement. I was committed, with no way to back out.

Step 5: Reach Out

A month went by and again I checked my savings; I was still behind, even with the raise. For the second time, I felt my dream starting to slip away. It was time to reach out. I drafted an email, shared my story with friends and asked for ideas and assistance. This was a difficult move for me, since I was raised with the mantra "God helps those who help themselves." Three days later, I was offered a job to work for my hero at the time, motivational speaker Tony Robbins. I didn't see that one coming.

Step 6: Enroll Others in Your Dream

Three months into my grand experiment, I was working for Tony during the week, and I was still doing my original work with autistic children part-time on the weekends. I was steaming ahead towards my goal and things were looking up. By May 15th, my savings account read $8500. I had three months to save $6500. Damn! I was still behind. I had cut all of my expenses as low as I could and I still wasn't saving enough. Again, I reached out with an email. The next day, an old boss of mine called with an offer to pay me $5000 dollars to teach wakeboarding and cover all my living expenses for the summer. Even though he was offering three times the normal pay, it still was not enough. I asked for $6500, and he agreed! "Just this one time, because I want to support your dream," he said.

After one of the best summers of my life, I finished my contract, went to Wells Fargo and deposited my last paycheck. My account balance read $15,023. The first call was to my father. "Dad I did it!" Three weeks later, I boarded a plane for China and began a nine-month journey around the world.

Looking back on that experience, even more important than the adventure itself is what I learned about the power of committing to a worthy goal. I had learned the formula, and never again did I not follow a dream because "I didn't have the money."

$0 to $100,000

A

FTER TRAVELING AROUND THE WORLD, I secretly wondered if my new "success formula" was just a one hit wonder or something I could replicate. Years later, I again found myself with an empty bank account, exhausted by my work as a teacher and desperately wanting to start a new business. I thought I would put my formula to the test. I borrowed $6000 to be coached by Martha Beck, a woman who at that time was considered to be one of the better life coaches in the country. I was making $18 an hour, so $6000 seemed like a huge sum of money. I knew she was a powerful coach and figured at the bare minimum, I would earn my investment back. During our short but intense time together, I declared that I would make $100,000 after taxes and launch my business in the next 1½ years! To the people around me, my proclamation seemed naive, especially considering I wanted to make such a huge leap without any kind of a plan. Martha even confided in me years later that she thought I was aiming too high, but she kindly kept it to herself.

After returning home, I followed step two of my formula and shared my vision with everyone who would listen. I really didn't know *how* I would accomplish my goal, only that it was deeply important, and that I would find a way. The "why" was the most important part of my No Plan-Plan.

Two months later, my future was again altered by a huge disaster. This time it was not the work of terrorists, but the wrath of Mother Nature. Hurricane Katrina had slammed into the Gulf Coast, wreaking havoc and creating a huge mess that needed to be cleaned up. As I watched the events unfold on television, I got a knock on my door. It was my neighbor Tim. "Jesse, I have an amazing opportunity I want to tell you about! I'm quitting my job and moving to Florida. They are hiring 5000 new insurance adjusters and you can make all kinds of money." My first thought was that it must be a scam. But then again, what if it wasn't? What if this was the break I had been looking for?" For days, I flip-flopped back and forth between unbridled excitement, fear and doubt. I played out hundreds of different scenarios, fully experiencing the joy of success and the agony of defeat over and over in my mind and body. I had heard that the mind didn't know the difference between the truth and a well-imagined fantasy, and I was living proof.

I sat on the fence for days, agonizing. Give up my entire life on a whim? No guarantee, not even a contract? It was the most thrilling and terrifying offer I had ever had. What if it wasn't real and I had to return home with my tail between my legs, with no job and no place to live? Days later, my neighbor was gone, his apartment was empty and the energy of possibility was gone along with him.

I started to slip into deep regret. I had chickened out. I had missed my chance. Then my phone rang, and it was Tim. "Jesse, we are here! It's real! They just gave us $1,500 checks just for showing up! They are talking about us making ten to fifteen thousand a month! Call this number, do whatever you have to do to speak with Gene. She's the person who hired me. Don't quit until you get her on the phone!" Adrenaline surged through my body. This was it! This was how I was going to get start-up money for my business!"

Determined to make it happen, I dialed the number. The line was busy. I called again, and all circuits were full. I called again and got a real person who put me on hold and never picked back up. Thousands of people were calling in, scrambling for these positions. I called over a hundred times, getting busy signals, hang-ups and speaking to dozens of different temp workers who had been hired to filter calls. "Do you have an appointment?" they would ask. "Have you gone through the preliminary interview? Do you have experience?" If I stuttered on an answer they would put me on hold or flat out tell me no. My desperation morphed into sheer determination.

The phone picked up. "This is Jesse Gros again, I *must* speak to Gene, I have quit my job, I'm ready to deploy and I will not be placed on hold again. I know you can help me."

The operator answered, "Of course, why didn't you just say so?" I heard a click.

"This is Gene." A chill ran through my body. She could have been Ed McMahon, telling me I had just won a million dollars. My mother's words rang through my ears. *The less you say, the better.* I took a deep breath and said in a measured voice,

"Gene, I'm ready to deploy." Pause. Silence.

"That's great, Jesse, well then you don't need to talk to me, talk to my secretary, and she'll get you set up." I had just somehow skipped the entire interview process. I pushed mute on the phone and danced around the living room, pumping my fists like a fanatic soccer fan.

Click. "Please don't drop the call," I pleaded in my mind. "Hi Jesse, I'm Gene's assistant, um, we have a little problem." *Party's over,* I thought. "I don't see your paperwork in the system." Stay calm. I'm screwed. Here comes the turnaround. My mouth opened and before I could think, I started talking.

"You *lost* my paperwork?! Do you know what I have been through to be ready to take this job?" I held my breath.

"I am so sorry Mr. Gros. I have no idea what happened."

"I do. I need this to happen!" *Don't say anything,* I thought. Silence. I could hear her fingers on the keyboard. More silence. "Mr. Gros, I can fix this. Here's what I'm going to do for you. I'm going to send you an application. Fill it out quickly, email it right back to me and I'll do the rest." My heart was pounding.

"Now that we have that handled, what about my girlfriend?"

"I don't see her in here either." Silence. Again my mother's voice. *The less you say the better.*

"Don't you worry about her, Jesse, I'll take care of you both. Things are so crazy around here. I am so sorry for the inconvenience. Your paperwork will clear tonight. You need to be in Tallahassee, Florida in five days at the Hilton on Apalachee Parkway, 10AM sharp. Welcome to the family. Bye, Jesse."

The phone went dead.

Five days later, we stood in a hotel lobby with hundreds of other new recruits just like us. All of us had left our jobs, families and lives on a moment's notice to drive halfway across the country for hopes of a better life. It felt like the gold rush, only this time it was all happening in the South.

I worked long hours seven days a week helping the people of Louisiana try to put their lives back together. The company I worked for was extremely generous with their customers and we were strongly encouraged to look for ways to pay them for their losses. They were also very generous with their employees and they paid us well.

Fifteen months later, I returned home with $100,000 in my account. I fired an email off to my coach. "Mission accomplished."

People Are Messy

WE ARE VERY MESSY PEOPLE. As a child, people called me Messy Jesse in school. I loved to run around shirtless and barefoot playing in the mud. I would often get in trouble at school for not wanting to wear shoes in class. I loved making mud pies, digging tunnels and creating worlds out of dirt and twigs. I would put hundreds of roly polies in my mouth and roll them around to spit out into pile and watch them unroll and craw away, to the horror of any adults watching. Besides how neat they felt in my mouth all rolled up, I think getting the reaction was half the fun.

But of course this chapter is not about roly polies. It's about humans. It's about how we are messy people. We have emotions, out of control monkey brains, changing desires, shifting moods and complicated interactions. It's been said that our communication with each other is only really accurate about twenty percent of the time. Yes, we are messy people.

This is a beautiful thing, though. How boring would life be if we were all clean and tidy and in control? So, I say, let's embrace our messiness and stop trying to be perfect. One of my favorite movie characters of all time is Tyler Durden (if you couldn't tell already from the multiple references) from the movie *Fight Club*. If you have not seen it, it's a deeply spiritual movie, (though this is not obvious by the title). In the movie, the lead character, played by Ed Norton, lives a life of quiet desperation. He hates his job, works long hours and comes home alone every night to clean his condo. Flipping through an IKEA catalog he wonders, "What kind of dining set defines me as a person?" He is lost in the dull life of unfulfilling work and consumption.

Later in the movie, his apartment catches fire and blows up. Everything is gone. Sitting in a bar with his new friend Tyler, he says, "I had it all, I had a stereo that was very decent, a wardrobe that was very respectable. I was close to being complete." Tyler offers his condolences: "Shit man, now it's all gone." He then launches into his manifesto:

"We are consumers, we are byproducts of a lifestyle obsession.

"I say never be complete,

"I say stop being perfect.

"I say let's evolve, let the chips fall where they may."

Later in the film, Tyler suggests that the goal is to "hit rock bottom," in direct violation of the pull of popular culture. In essence, he meant letting go of attachments to vanity, perfectionism and consumerism, etc., in order to live a more purpose-filled, free life. The characters are learning to embrace themselves as messy and imperfect. As the scene fades away...you know that they go on to create something big.

In my early years, I had beautiful visions of perfection for my life and there was no space for me in them. No space for messy Jesse to show up. No room for mistakes. No room for creativity either.

So, rather than mess up my beautiful images by starting my business, I just sat on them and allowed them to live perfectly in the sky, while I suffered in the background.

A client of mine who was building her coaching practice shared some thoughts with me one day about her first workshop. She said that many of the women connected deeply, shared intimately and opened up. She was very pleased about this. "And," she shared, "it was very unpolished." As if that was a bad thing.

"Good." I said. "Tell me more."

"The evening felt raw and I was very honest with the group about how I was feeling during the experiences. How can I polish this up?" she asked.

"Don't!" I said. "Keep it raw, keep it honest. If you want people to share openly and let their guard down, then you lead by sharing openly and letting your guard down."

She has decided to go with her raw and unpolished self, and she tells her clients this ahead of time. "This workshop is going to be spontaneous, free and most likely a wild ride. Who's coming with me?"

Celebrate the Imbalanced Life

HOW OFTEN HAVE YOU HEARD PEOPLE talking about a balanced life? For years I subscribed to this idea. A balanced life, a balanced life, someday I will have it. Someday I will get *there*. Like it was a state of being that was attainable over a long period of time. Maybe it was possible for Buddha, but not me. I have had moments of what I would call a balanced life, but they've never seemed to last very long.

I realized that I have been off balance for most of my life, like a plane constantly correcting course over time to get to its destination. Or, like the stock market zigzagging up and down daily, but smoothing out if you look at it over a long enough timeline. That's what I wanted in my life all along...a nice smooth growth over time. But often I am so in the moment that I experience the growth as steep ups filled with joy, and the challenges as steep drops filled with "not-joy." In these situations, I don't feel balanced, and yet I'm very engaged in my life.

Looking back, when I was freewheeling around the world, I had a huge amount of free time, but less money and less of a sense accomplishment. I was off balance. Then, when I came back and was working 100-hour workweeks in the insurance business, I had lots of money, no free time and a sense of pride for a job well done. Again, I was off balance. Then there was the time I was surfing almost every day for 2-5 hours a day - a dream life some would say. However, I was not moving forward to pursue my career and it weighed on me.

Even the gurus find themselves living an unbalanced life. A writer friend of mine joked about the long hours Tim Ferriss, author of *The 4-Hour Workweek,* was putting in on his second book. I found this a bit ironic and yet very similar to my personal experience.

So, what to do? I was stuck, judging myself for not being able to create the long-term state of blissful balance that I read about in so many self-help books. I had to come to terms with the fact that I am too creatively impulsive to live a nice, evenly proportioned life. So I gave up the illusion of the balanced life and breathed in a deep sigh of relief. I have a beautifully imbalanced life and I love it! Sometimes I work too much, sometimes I play too much, sometimes I eat too much, sometimes I sleep too much...but never have I danced too much. Well... maybe one time.

> *Everything in moderation, especially moderation.*
> **— Anonymous**

I am choosing to live my life according to the wisdom of the Rubik's Cube. No, it's not a new cult or iPhone app. It's something that came to me in a dream after a long day of snowboarding. What if life is like a Rubik's Cube? All six sides represent our core values: family, health, career, spiritual connection, service, etc., and we strive to have each side all lined up. However, if you have ever tried to complete a Rubik's Cube, it's a very difficult feat. Just when you get one color all lined up (for example your financial life), you realize that you have messed up the green and blue sides that only three turns ago were complete! UGH!! Now you settle on yellow. It looks really good. You wonder if you can just line up another side without messing this side up. And on and on you go, constantly upsetting the parts of your life that you had "all figured out" in an effort to get all the sides lined up and complete. Personally, I have never completed a Rubik's Cube and I can't imagine I'll ever have all of the parts of my life perfectly lined up.

Fear of Failure and Money Delusions

BEFORE I STARTED MY CAREER in the insurance business, I thought my biggest block to success as a coach was money. I couldn't help but think, "Who would hire a life coach who has never been financially successful?" (Regardless of my education, abilities or certifications.) I had it in my mind that if I earned six figures, I would be worthy and people would listen.

Fifteen months after my first assignment as an insurance adjuster, I returned home with my financial mission accomplished. Surely I could now start my coaching practice in a powerful way. Two weeks after returning home, I slipped into a funk. How could this be? I had accomplished my goal. I had proved that I was a "successful man" in my mind. Yet, I was still scared to really put myself out there and coach. I found myself in almost the same place emotionally as I had been before I left. Only now, I was not just a scared guy, but a scared guy with savings. I couldn't believe how quickly the buzz wore off from the money. It turned out money could not fill the hole in my self-esteem. Damn!

For months, I struggled to gain traction and start my business. I could feel the momentum just starting to pick up and then I was called back to insurance work. "We have another big contract for you!" they said. I could feel the thrill of the potential money I could earn and the rush that comes with the arrival of a new storm. Hurricane Rita had made landfall, and the message on my phone said, "We need you here in 24 hours."

Again I up-ended my life and took off across the country. *Maybe I'll do just one more contract, then I'll really have enough money,* I thought. That moment of feeling like I had enough money never came, though, and I continued to work as an adjuster for the next three years. Over time, the emotional intensity of working in disaster zones and the pace of the work took its toll on me. The money became a bit of an addiction, and the more I worked, the more I felt like I was moving away from my dreams. At the end, I started having panic attacks at work. I would walk into a burned-out building, my heart would start to thump, my chest would constrict and my throat would tighten. Every part of my body was telling me, "Run!"

One day, while jogging before work, I heard Obama giving a rousing speech about choosing a career with meaning and purpose. Tears streamed down my face as I ran. I couldn't take it anymore. That night I called my boss and told him I was done. "Are you sure?" he said. "There are a lot of people in line who want your position."

My voice cracked. "Yes, I'm sure." I knew more money was not going to get me over my fear of failure. I just had to jump in and do it. Six months later, my new coaching website went live and I led my first Insight Adventures™ retreat to Mexico.

Since that day, I have never again worked "for the money."

Change the World?
(How Much Is Enough?)

If there is light in the soul,
there is beauty in the person.
If there is beauty in the person,
there is harmony in the house.
If there is harmony in the house,
there is order in the nation.
If there is order in the nation,
there will be peace on earth.
— Chinese Proverb

HOW DO YOU KNOW IF YOU ARE making a difference in the world? Does it have to be big? How would you know if big is big enough? How many people do you have to influence to know you are making a big enough difference in the world?

I found myself asking these same questions and felt ashamed of my answer. *No, I am not doing enough for the world,* I thought. *I should be doing more. Why? Because if I was,* then *I would know my life was meaningful.* It was during a call on a radio show hosted by Dr. Ron and Dr. Mary Hulnick that I gained some clarity about this idea of how much is enough.

I called into the radio show and explained that I had been watching TED Talks online and I was deeply impacted by what I saw. People were using their creativity and enthusiasm in big ways to change the world. I was comparing myself with them and felt horrible, like I just wasn't doing enough.

Dr. Hulnick responded, "How much is enough? How many people do you have to help to know that you are doing enough? What's your magic number?" His questions caught me off guard and I stumbled on my response. I didn't have a specific number, just a feeling of inadequacy.

Mary chimed in, "What I hear is that it's something inside you that is feeling 'not enough' and that you are seeking to fill that gap through your work. That method is not going to give you what you are looking for." She recommended that I check inside and see what judgments I had about myself and the work I was doing. I needed to start by working on healing those judgments from the inside.

I had been looking outside of me for validation and had slipped into a kind of imagined responsibility to "help the world." I fantasized that if I was one of the people on TED Talks, I would feel whole and complete.

Dr. Hulnick continued, "The only responsibility you have in this lifetime is to your own upliftment and growth. If you only ever worked on being a loving compassionate person and healing your own unresolved material, that would be enough."

If we each take responsibility for our own healing and focus on that, the world would be a very different place.

He who cannot first master himself is never truly a master regardless of what castles he has built or empires created.
— **Anonymous**

I Want to Give It All Away

THE FIRST TIME I HAD A LOT of financial success, I was plagued for several years by this powerful feeling that I wanted to lose my money or just give it all away. I'm not a big gambler, and yet I had visions of going to Vegas and putting it all on black. Several times, I almost gave it all away to charity. Rather than going to Vegas, I did the next closest thing; I took a large chunk of my savings and invested it in a single stock. Five days later, the stock value dropped in half. When I heard the news, a feeling of warmth and safety came over me. It was very strange. I tried to wrap my head around this odd experience, but couldn't figure out why my mind was scared and yet my body was sending me clear signals of safety.

During this time, I experienced a mix of emotions. I felt embarrassed that I had so much while others were barely making it through the week. I also felt separation from my friends who were still struggling with their careers. Sometimes I could feel their envy and it felt horrible. I had worked so hard, and yet there I sat, feeling empty and disconnected from myself and others. The bottom line was that some part of me felt that like having this money would separate me from love.

In truth, the only thing creating any kind of separation was my misunderstanding about money and about myself. I had it linked up that money = loneliness and separation. And while I was an insurance adjuster, that was very much my experience. I was living away from my friends and family, often in places that felt totally foreign to me.

So how did I heal this, and not just give away, spend or lose all of my savings? I got to work on my dream. I started getting paid to coach and lead retreats. Once I was getting paid for something I really believed in, the link that money = separation and loneliness was broken. It was replaced by money = exchange for service and fun. For me, coaching and leading retreats is service and it's damn fun!

P.S. That stock I told you about – I held onto it for five years and had all but forgotten about it, assuming my money was gone. As I was writing this chapter, I pulled it up online to check on it for the first time since the huge drop. It had gone back up to over fifty percent the original purchase price! I sold the stock and felt the same warm buzz I did the first time when it had tanked five years before. It looks like my intuition had been ahead of my mind the whole time.

A Conscious Business in Action

A GOOD FRIEND OF MINE, JANE, has a thriving yoga studio in Los Angeles. In talking to her about building her business, I asked her why she thought the previous owners did not succeed. She shared with me that their main goal was to make money. They had no background in yoga and really were not that connected to it. They set out to "create a lucrative" (basically soulless) business. "This may work for selling cars, but not for yoga," she shared.

Jane shared with me that the day she took over the business, new teachers and students started showing up almost out of thin air. This was before she had done any new marketing or made any changes to the studio. The only thing that shifted was that she was now the anchor for the energy and mission of the studio. I had walked past the studio for over a year and had always felt that it looked a bit uninviting. After Jane took over, I suddenly felt compelled to come in. Yet from the outside there was nothing different I could "see."

One of the things that I immediately noticed was the overall energy of the studio. When I was there it felt like home. I didn't feel like I was just another customer to be marketed to and sold to. I also noticed the ease and grace that Jane brought to the more challenging parts of her business.

Six months after Jane's grand opening, the tenant above her decided that she wanted to expand her store into part of the yoga studio. She found an error in the lease contract and it turned out that both she and Jane had rights to the same corner of the building. She threatened the landlord and Jane with legal action if they did not go along with her demands.

I asked Jane if she was fighting back. She shared that she could, but it would probably get ugly and it was not worth it to bring that energy into her studio, even if it meant losing a part of her space. A part of me wanted her to fight this bully, but I soon realized that she was not just running a yoga studio, but bringing the yogic way of living into all aspects of her business.

To avoid the fight and keep the energetic integrity of her studio (and her own life), Jane let the other tenant take over the extra space. The loss of space inspired Jane to create a whole new lounge area that she had been putting off for months. I watched the whole process and I was inspired by how she moved through it with such ease and grace. I realized that Jane was not only teaching yoga, but also truly living it.

After living abroad for several years in yogic practice, Jane is now bringing her deep level of respect for the sacred practice of yoga and her business skills into what I see as a beautiful model of a conscious business. One visit and you can tell something special is going on there.

Bringing Love to Business

I've heard people say that they cling to their painful thoughts because they're afraid that without them they wouldn't be activists for peace. "If I feel peaceful," they say, "why would I bother taking action at all?"

My answer is "Because that's what love does." To think that we need sadness or outrage to motivate us to do what's right is insane. As if the clearer and happier you get, the less kind you become. As if when someone finds freedom, she just sits around all day with drool running down her chin.

My experience is the opposite.

Love is action.
— Byron Katie

I F YOU HAD TOLD ME FIVE YEARS AGO that building a conscious business was about love, I would have smiled at you and thought, *Sure it is, until it's time to pay the bills.* Having made my way up through the very competitive environments of school, sports and later a commission-only career, I was pretty damn sure that creating a business was about being better than those around me. When I was pre-med, I looked at every person in my class as competition, someone in the way of my future, someone who had to lose in order for me to win. In my insurance work, the top closers got to keep their jobs while everyone else got laid off.

For the first several years of building my coaching practice, I did it from my old model of scarcity and competition. I thought of other coaches and of people in my field as competition, not as peers. I had many people want to partner with me and I turned them all down out of fear that they would try to take something from me. When someone else in my community would offer a retreat in the same month as one of mine, I would get angry and scared, thinking that they would somehow "steal" *my* clients. I claimed to be operating a conscious business, but my love and respect was really only reserved for my clients and friends.

> *Power, Fame & Glory are Junk Food for the Soul:*
> *Cheap substitutes for love, belonging and purpose.*
> **— Dr. Logan**

Aware of my own hypocrisy, I felt trapped in a constant battle between my ego and my softer, more loving self. I had taken all of the courses and read the books, but I still found it very difficult to leave my old model of working. Deep down, I had a fear that if I stopped competing for what seemed to be limited resources and adopted a more conscious, loving approach based on service, I would lose my edge. I had this image in my head of becoming some kind of a flakey, new age, semi-homeless person, wandering around loving everyone and everything and sleeping on my friends' couches forever.

It did not take long to learn that I was not the only person thinking this way. Many of my clients had experienced the same fears:

Dr. Ron is an extremely high achieving professional who left his corporate career to start an alternative health business. His goal is to help hundreds of millions of people in his lifetime. If there is one person I know who can make this happen, it's him.

While he was growing his new practice, he found that he was building it in an unconscious way. He was operating out of scarcity, ego and competition. I offered up to him a different model. I said: "What if you build your organization solely focused on being of service to others, rather than trying to be the 'best.'" I knew this would be a stretch because a large part of his self-concept was wrapped up in winning.

"Ok, I'll give it a try," he agreed. Many months later, his organization was growing quickly, but he was still operating in many of the same old ways. He was attaching his value as a person to his accomplishments. "I want to build something huge, something that really makes a difference. At the end of my life, I want to know I matter," he said.

"What if you just mattered right now? What if you could find love for yourself right now, in this moment and it had nothing to do with your accomplishments? What if you just appreciated yourself as you are and built this movement out of respect for the people you are helping, rather than out of an attempt to prove your worthiness as a human being on the planet?" His response offered up the answer to my own resistance that I had been feeling for some time.

"I'm afraid that if I were to just love myself as I am and build the business coming from service and a loving place, I'll lose my desire to achieve and just sit around doing nothing, being perfectly content."

Without the motivating factors of fear of failure and imagined feelings of significance through success, he was afraid he would cease to act. And this was the very excuse that I had used for years to convince myself that this *love stuff* really didn't deserve a large place in a successful business.

After we completed our year of working together, I asked Dr. Ron what he felt he had learned. I wanted to know if love and service had found a place in his business. He shared with me that in his line of work there are very few people that truly understand what he's trying to accomplish. He used to feel very alone in his mission, he said, but recently things had changed.

When my actions are driven by ego, I feel alone. When driven by service - when really authentic - it doesn't seem to matter.
— **Dr. Ron**

I reached my own mental tipping point about the role of love in business in a conversation with a very successful healer friend of mine named David Elliot. He shared with me a story that was indicative of how he ran both his practice and life. Before he was a healer, he worked as a construction contractor. He would look at the work that needed to be done on a particular job, and then a price would just pop into his head and that was his quote. Using this method, he won almost 100 percent of his bids. His peers said that he should be measuring by square feet, and that according to the *experts*, if he was charging enough, he should be getting rejected about thirty percent of the time. "Clearly, you must be doing something wrong," they said. David ignored the *experts* and continued to follow his intuition and did very well.

He said to me one day, in a very matter of fact way, "You know with my healing work, I don't really advertise." He doesn't offer promos, or "buy now" deals or even talk about his other events or offerings, at the end of a session. There is not an ounce of fear or scarcity that I have ever detected in the years I have worked with him. And, looking at his schedule, he is booked for the year! Leading with love has not stifled his ability to be successful one bit.

I shifted the way I was relating to my business. When I noticed fear trying to creep in, I just reminded myself that there was no scarcity of potential people I could help. There are hundreds of millions of people in the world who have a deep a desire to make powerful changes in their lives.

Someone asked me the other day, "So tell me, who's your competition and how are you positioning yourself in your market?" I just stared at him for a while, and for a moment I felt confused by the question.

"I have no competition," I answered. And I truly meant it.

Saved by the Pizza Man

ABOUT TWO YEARS into my coaching practice, I found myself in a deep slump. I had not signed on any new clients for months and my retreat to Nepal had not one signup. I was deeply questioning myself. *Maybe this was all just a pipe dream,* I thought. *Maybe I'm an idiot for quitting my career. Damn this* following your dreams stuff. *Damn this positive thinking crap.* And there I got stuck for months, plodding along, doing all the things I thought I was supposed to be doing, and my dreams were not coming together as planned. So what did I do?

I gallantly turned it all around, doves flew in the air and trumpets played in the distance. No, that's not what happened. I did what any self-respecting disappointed person does: I found other disappointed people to commiserate with who had also left their careers to pursue their dreams. And together we complained and came up with conspiracy theories about how we had been duped by the self-help industry into believing that we could actually follow our dreams and have careers that we loved. The shame of it all!

Was it really possible? Or was it all just a pipe dream for those chosen few who end up on Oprah looking wonderful and happy as they blab about getting paid to do Feng Shui for movie stars and teaching Drew Barrymore how to bend spoons. *Maybe all of these successful coaches and healers are in it together, making money on selling us a dream that doesn't even exist,* I thought. That was my favorite theory.

Coming to the conclusion that I couldn't stay in this place forever, I finally made my move. "I'm going to be really bold and brave. I am going to crack the code of this mystery. I'm going to quit! Yes...that will solve my problems! Along with the people who refuse to vote, I will be a conscientious objector! The system is rigged, so why play anyway. Besides, I'm an artist and this wasn't really for me anyway."

I needed one more person to listen to me and help me justify my quitting, so I called my close friend and invited myself over for a long lunch. For hours I lay there on the couch with my head on the pillow, talking to her like I was in an old school therapist's office. I explained to her how the system was rigged and built my case for why quitting was really my best option. After a while, my body started to go numb and I got dizzy. Time to hit the eject button. "Hey, can we go out to lunch now?" I said.

We went to small family owned pizza place and I got some comfort food in my system. I leaned over to my friend and said, "I feel better now. And as I was saying...let me give you ten more good reasons I should quit." Halfway through my list, the owner of the restaurant appeared at our table.

"What's this about you wanting to quit your business?" he asked me point blank. I looked at him, a bit stunned.

"Pardon me for eavesdropping, but I couldn't help but butt in," he continued. You know, this is my restaurant. Twice in my life, I have considering quitting and walking away. So you know what I did? I changed it and made it work for me! You don't work for your business, *it works for you.* Don't quit, you are just starting out. Whatever you don't like, change it."

And with a smile, he was gone, like something out of a made-for-TV movie.

I felt chills up my arms. "Did that just happen?" I asked out loud.

"Sure did," she replied. There was a long silence. "If that's not divine intervention, I don't know what is," she said. After lunch, I marched straight home and got busy recreating my business in a way that worked for *me*.

Keep it Simple

The hardest thing in life is to keep it simple.
— **Thomas Dunn**

EVEN THOUGH HE DIED before I was born, my grandfather Dunn taught me a lot. As a lawyer in rural Pennsylvania in the 1930's, he was aware of how the complexities in life have a tendency to pile up and rob us of our peace. He was equally aware that indeed, we have a choice.

Since the 1930's, life has become increasingly complex and the work of keeping it simple even a more daunting task. The simple fact that I have over thirty passwords to remember as part of my everyday living is telling. I even read once that there was a nervous disorder linked to people having too many passwords and login codes.

Human beings have a very difficult time actually creating freedom for themselves. We will build elaborate systems that take enormous care and feeding. So that you have absolutely no time for you own silence. And you have no time for your own imaginative experience. And for the radical simplicities it takes to keep an attentive and watchful heart in the world.
— **David Whyte, English poet**

In an attempt to keep my life as simple as possible without just completely checking out and moving to a cabin in the woods (which I did do for two months during the writing of this book), I created a simple question that all new additions to my personal and work life are subjected to:

"Will this new (friendship, Web App, training), make my life simpler? And, if it adds complexity, it is worth it?"

Most of the time my answer is NO.

In one two-hour session with a potential client, I realized that he was going to be very high maintenance and require a lot of attention. I chose not to work with him and turned down many thousands of dollars, based on my simple filter. The choice was easy.

I find keeping my life as simple as possible allows me to walk through life with an open heart and connect with people on a level that opens theirs as well.

Intuition Internship

Your time is limited, don't waste it living someone else's life.
Don't be trapped by dogma, which is living the result of other
people's thinking. Don't let the noise of others' opinions drown
your own inner voice. And most important, have the courage to
follow your heart and intuition, they somehow already know
what you truly want to become. Everything else is secondary.
— Steve Jobs

HOW OFTEN HAS INTUITION played a part in your life? How often do you listen? Do you know how to connect to your intuition? Or as a teacher of mine once asked, "What part of your intuition are you ignoring?"

Many times in the early years of building my coaching business, intuition served me well. And it still does! Learning to tap into it on a regular basis is a worthwhile pursuit. One of the ways I have learned to connect to my intuition is through meditation and Breathwork. It was during one solo breathing session in my living room that I had a very strong hit to get an intern. Mid-session I jumped up, feeling dizzy and ethereal. I immediately posted on Facebook that I was looking for an intern.

This was something I had been putting off for two years. Within ten minutes, I had several responses. One of them was a young woman who had been my lead actress in a children's play I directed 14 years earlier. When I saw her response, I remembered thinking so many years before that someday we would work together again, and here she was. Katie was now a mother and looking for a meaningful project to do from home. We worked together for a year and she ended up being a wonderful addition to the team.

Masculine & Feminine Energy
at Work

FOR YEARS I HAD A VERY DIFFICULT TIME getting focused enough to build a business. I bounced from one project to the next. I was the guy with all kinds of great ideas, and not much follow-through, unless I had a very rigid structure. Being my own boss was likely to be a huge challenge!

Looking at my work patterns from the perspective of masculine vs. feminine energy was extremely helpful.

Spiritual energy, by nature, connects through the feminine - soft, creative and open to receiving. Masculine energy is all about doing and getting things done. Along my journey I discovered that I have very strong masculine and feminine energies. I love the process of dreaming, scheming and talking about grand visions. It's there that I connect to my intuition and source my creativity. As much as I would love to stay in the place of creation all of the time, I shift into my masculine energy when it's time to do the work that will make the vision a reality. It's this part of me that keeps things on task, doesn't back down from roadblocks and stays on the phone all week until a retreat is filled.

I used to bounce back and forth between these energies, trying to find my center, judging my feminine side as too dreamy and flaky and my masculine side as spiritually disconnected and harsh. It felt like I had a small war going on inside, battling for control. It never occurred to me that I didn't have to choose a side. After a session with a coach friend of mine, we came to a brilliant solution. "Why not run full-speed in both directions?" he suggested. At first this idea felt bizarre to me. It felt like I would be stretched out, like I was on a medieval torture rack. I chose to give it a try and it has worked out that embracing both sides has indeed stretched me, but I haven't broken. It has allowed me to expand and embrace my full range as a person.

I have also learned to better distinguish what kind of energy is most appropriate for the task at hand. For example, a dream of mine for years had been to delegate most of the major responsibilities that come with leading two-week long international retreats. As you can imagine, there are a lot of moving parts. What I have noticed over the years, in my attempt to wear many different hats, is that it's easy to fall into being efficient and productive but emotionally unavailable. This works great for logistics, planning and running the trip. However, I noticed that it interfered with my ability to show up fully present for my clients.

You can't be efficient with people.
— **Stephen Covey**

Every year, I have delegated more and more of my duties; things I am really good at, but that keep me in my masculine energy. This is something that's very difficult to do for a person who traditionally would just "do it all." I have now reached the point where all of the logistics of the outer journey are being handled by others, so that I can focus on the inner journey with my clients. For me, this is the ultimate gift – staying open in the creative energy of the feminine, flow and connection to spirit.

Calling in Your Tribe

THE GREATEST LEARNING in the last twenty years for me has been the realization that *I don't have to do it alone.* Surrounding myself with like-minded, open-hearted people and eliciting their support has completely changed my experience of myself and those around me. It has allowed me to relax out of deep, old patterns of survival and lean into the safety of community.

Have you found your people? Do the people who you spend your life with inspire you? Do you feel your energy surge in their presence? Do they encourage you to show up as the greatest version of yourself?

You may have had the experience in high school, in college or as part of a team when you felt like you were with *your people.* You worked together in person on a shared goal that brought you closer, creating a strong sense of community.

Once I left the bubble of school, I felt my intimate connections slip and fade away into the shallow sphere of social media. I brought this idea up with friends and clients and it seemed many people had just accepted the loss of intimacy as a natural part of growing up. It seems as though the business world is not set up to help maintain and foster more than a few meaningful relationships.

Consider what's possible: what if you had many friends with whom you shared your love, vulnerability and dreams? What if the level of connection and support you experience now is only a small fraction of what is available to you?

It may be time to deepen your current relationships and expand your circle of friends.

The best way to start is to look at the people already in your world. Is there anyone who you would like to get to know better or more intimately? Are there parts of you that are still unexpressed? Are there pieces of yourself that you could get to know more intimately?

The part of me that is yearning to be expressed is:

_____

The part of me that I would love to get to know better is:

_____

The person I know who I would like to get to know better is:

_____

Once you have looked at yourself and those already in your tribe, it's time to venture outward. Start your search by going to the places where people that inspire you go: conferences, festivals, trainings, workshops and Meet-ups. These places are magnets for people with similar interests who are brought together to connect with each other over a shared passion or interest. The very nature of these events creates a filter to bring people together who are more likely to connect on a deeper level. There, you can take risks to connect with people and discover opportunities to develop friendships based on your common interests and passions. Research shows that the greatest indicator for people becoming friends is proximity. Simply being in the physical space of the people you want to be around is the best predictor that you will connect with them and soon become part of a larger tribe.

On an unexpected personal journey of discovery in 2011, I went to the Telluride Mountain Film Festival. I had always felt pulled to this event, but I had never gone because I thought it would somehow pull me off-track. When I arrived I immediately felt like I was home. Walking around I had this bizarre and yet comfortable feeling that I had met almost everyone there before. The town was full of adventurers, filmmakers and environmentalists. I admired all of these people from a distance, yet never considered myself to be one of them - even after I was guiding trips to Nepal!

While I was there, my energy surged. Any natural shyness was gone and I met dozens of amazing filmmakers, skiers and passionate environmentalists. I was deeply inspired by their stories and their work. I made more new friends in four days than I had in the past year! I was in the flow, surrounded by my "tribe," my people. I went on to work with several of the extreme skiers, made friends with the filmmakers from the electric car movement and even managed to get a large donation of winter coats from The North Face® to support our work with young women in rural Nepal.

I find it ironic that for so long I resisted going to this festival. I was afraid that I would get wrapped up in the free wheeling mountain culture and get off- track. The truth is, this short adventure expanded my tribe in directions I never could have anticipated.

The Dream Becomes Reality

WALKING DOWN A NARROW COBBLESTONE street, soaking wet, I had a huge smile on my face. Caught in a sudden rainstorm without cover, I embraced my plight, splashing in the water, walking straight down the middle of street. Water poured off the stucco roofs like small waterfalls, turning the tiny avenues into small rivers and the entire city into a huge cascading cobblestone water fountain. Everywhere people scurried to get under shelter.

Under the dark clouds, the city looked beautiful and mysterious. I marveled at the fact that the 300-year-old buildings that lined the streets still kept their occupants warm and safe, despite years of erosion and being pounded by thousands of tropical rainstorms. I was having so much fun in the moment that I soon lost my way. I stepped into a little shop to call my hotel. "You are very close," the woman on the phone reassured me. "Only 15 minutes walking. Would you like me to light the fire in your room Mr. Gros?" "Si Senora!" Now *that* was an idea!

I eventually found my way back to my little boutique hotel and the "staff" stood waiting at the door. I could see her smiling at me, trying not to laugh. "No umbrellas Mr. Gros?" Laura, the manager/head chef/bell person asked. "It was sunny when I left!" I protested. She laughed as I rung my shirt out on the front step. "From now on you take umbrellas Mr. Gros." Laura shoved her umbrella into my hand. I loved being soaked, playing in the warm rain...I was so happy to *not* have my umbrellas.

Now out of the rain, but very much still in the storm, I again stared at the volume of water pouring off the roof into the open courtyard. Joined by the sounds of the heavy drops pounding on the metal roof and building-shaking claps of thunder, the entire scene was exhilarating.

In my room the fire was already roaring. I laid my wet socks by the hearth and they immediately started to steam. I put on my pjs, made a hot cup of tea and flopped into a plush chair by the fire. From there I sat and watched the rain come down on the city.

Having just arrived in Antigua I had several coaching calls to do, then the rest of a week was mine to explore on my own, before my clients arrived. An intrepid family of five had hired me to create a custom retreat for their family. Even though I had never been there, I recommended Guatemala. With the perfect mix of historical cities, jungle treks, adventure and enough ancient ruins to bore Indiana Jones, Guatemala would be perfect for them. And...just to keep the mother really happy, I rented a beautiful lakeside home complete with an Italian personal chef for several nights. Everyone needs a break from adventure now and then!

An hour went by, just sitting and watching. Lost in the moment, I heard a faint digital alarm in the distance. Beep, beep, beep. *Must be the neighbors clock or something,* I thought. A minute went by and when it didn't stop, I realized it was *my* alarm, reminding me I had a coaching call at 3PM, which for me was 4PM Guatemala time.

This was my first international coaching call, and I was nervous that the storm would affect the cell reception. I was also afraid that my client wouldn't be able to hear me over the noise of the rain. *Maybe I'll crawl under all my blankets and pillows and do the call in my own makeshift sound room,* I thought. My mind raced back to warnings from a coach friend of mine. "Don't tell your clients you are out of the country," he said. "They might feel like you are not *there* for them. "I'm not into lying," I explained. (*And besides I am there for them,* I thought. *Unless of course this international phone call doesn't come through.*)

Suddenly, as if someone had turned a huge water faucet off, the rain just stopped! Within minutes, the clouds started to clear and again the sun was shining. My phone rang and it was time to go to work. "The number you gave me is different than your usual number. Where are you, Jesse?" My client asked.

"I'll show you," I said. I snapped a photo of the city on my phone and hit send." A minute later she responded, "Wow! Awesome office!"

"Yes...this is our Guatemala branch," I joked. "Okay. Let's get to work. How can we make this call extremely useful for you?" As she thought about the answer....I was hit with a deep realization.

It was in that very moment living the dream that I had created in my goals journal so many years before. After all of my work, I had done it! I had created almost the exact picture that I had painted in my mind. I was getting paid to travel and coach, without an office...free from attachment, open to explore and serve in a way that was deeply meaningful to me!

ADVENTURE

Getting out of our day-to-day experience, away from the influences of our culture, friends and family, opens up huge possibilities for us to discover new things about ourselves. The act of physically leaving our comfort zone elicits the wilder parts of our nature that are often not called upon in everyday living.

Whether it's trekking in the Himalayas or exploring my own neighborhood, going on an adventure is the best way I know to get myself out of feeling stuck and into inspiration.

Great breakthroughs in life come from a deeper sense of vision and imagination that can often only be accessed when we get far enough away from what we know and slow down enough to access our own natural genius.

What you can plan is too small for you to live.
What you can live wholeheartedly will make plans enough for
the vitality hidden in your sleep.
— **David Whyte, English poet**

Gloves Off — a Story From India

ON THE FIRST LEG OF A NINE-MONTH TRIP around the world, I arrived in Calcutta, India by myself without a guidebook or much of a plan. Several years of working in a challenging career had left me feeling burnt out and in serious need of change. Exactly what I wanted from my adventure wasn't clear; I just knew I needed to feel alive again.

At the airport, I was greeted by dozens of screaming cab drivers all vying for my fare. I stood paralyzed in the hot sun and swirling dust, staring at the crowd with stories of unscrupulous cab drivers circling though my head. Scanning the mob, I caught the eye of young blonde woman waiting behind a police barricade. I rushed over to her and blurted, "Do you speak English? You look like you are waiting for someone. Do you live here? Can I catch a ride with you?"

"Um, yes, yes and... yes," she smiled. Her name was Amy. At 18 years old, she had left her rural home in Pennsylvania and had come to India by herself to work with the poor in Calcutta's slums. I was totally impressed. When we arrived at the Salvation Army Youth Hostel, we met her friends; young, optimistic volunteers from all over the world. John had been there for almost a year working in an orphanage; Tran was a nurse who offered up her skills to a local hospital and Amy ran an entire volunteer program!

The next morning, after a nerve-wracking 10-minute rickshaw ride through narrow and chaotic streets, Amy and I arrived at Mother Theresa's Home for the Dying. Inside, things were already moving at full speed, and I was immediately spotted by the lead volunteer, a wild-eyed German man, who ran over and ordered, "You will be carrying the men from their beds to the washroom and so forth. Go get ready." Before I could introduce myself, he was gone and I stood frozen looking around the large barren room with rows upon rows of the abandoned elderly of Calcutta. Lying in each of the simple beds was a little shell of a human being tucked away under wool blankets. The sight of open wounds and damaged limbs made my stomach turn but I tried to not let anyone see my shock, and I forced a smile on my face. I put on an apron, two sets of latex gloves, took a deep breath and began my duties.

One by one, I carried their frail little bodies into the bathing room. Like little frightened children, the old men clung to their mattresses, whimpering and protesting at being removed from their warm beds. In my arms the men felt like skeletons, with a thin layer of stretched out skin holding them together. I stared at the wall as I walked and tried to keep my composure. I thought about what Amy had told me on the drive back from the airport. "Some of the elderly at the home are brought to us and others we find in trash dumpsters and back street alleys. They are abandoned by their families when they can no longer be cared for." My stomach ached.

After the men were fed, bathed and back in bed, several of us were given a new job. As most of the men were bedridden, they needed to be massaged daily to avoid bedsores and to promote circulation. I overheard one of the nurses saying that the man in the corner, separated from the main rows of beds, would not live much longer. His name was Abdi and he had been found alone in a trash dumpster. I kneeled down next to him and smiled, but he looked away as if embarrassed to see me. I spoke to him softly, poured the oil onto my gloves and began to rub his legs. His body felt stiff and almost lifeless.

Again, I tried to catch his eye with a smile, but he just looked away. I wondered if maybe I was doing something wrong, and I looked around the room to see what the other volunteers were doing.

Like a small production line, they moved from patient to patient, quickly applying the oil with their latex gloves. I noticed the lead volunteer worked with his bare hands and I chose to do the same. I let my gloves drop on the floor so that Abdi could see them. Slowly, gently I rubbed his legs and his arms, then I moved to his neck and finally his scalp. I could feel the tension in his muscles release and his breathing slowed. Suddenly, something caught my eye and I stopped; a single tear welled up in his eye and rolled down his cheek. He turned his head towards me and our eyes met. His big, dark eyes sparkled with gratitude. My throat clenched up and I just cried my heart out. Tears ran down my face onto his and then it hit me: Abdi and the other men in the room were not just patients, but real human beings, with a story and a history; people who were sharing their final moments on the planet with us.

That afternoon, I walked back to the hostel alone, unafraid of the street dogs and beggars, exhausted, yet feeling more alive than I had in years. I promised myself that I would slow down when I returned home. I vowed to remove the protective layers that kept me from connecting with those whom I loved and those I had yet to know.

Sherpa Funeral

THIS IS A STORY WRITTEN BY DR. RUTH DUNN, one of the participants on our Nepal adventure in 2012:

Dr. Dunn's story:

I cannot remember a time when I did not want to go to Nepal. Names of Himalayan giants were familiar as a child from reading the spines of adult books: Everest, K2, Annapurna, Lhotse, Kanchenjunga. I wanted to see the mountains.

The afternoon haze lay over the Kathmandu valley, dulling the clear autumn sunshine. Surrounding hills retreated into the distance, obscuring the outlines of neat white farmhouses and terraced fields among the forests. We arrived at the end of an unconstructed, bone-jarring road that wound through chaotic streets and passed under an archway at the bottom of a hill. The Sherpa funeral site was located on the top of a small hill covered with trees stirring in the breeze, and we climbed the narrow steps to the summit together. Groups of young Nepali men gathered quietly in the courtyard and a few children played among the crowd, oblivious to the naked grief on the faces of the family. The low chanting of monks drew their eyes to a covered enclosure at one end where the funeral rites were already underway. The body lay almost unnoticed on a pallet on the ground at the cremation site, covered by silk prayer scarves. As we talked in subdued tones, not wanting to be the obvious outsiders that we were, young Nepali women distributed cups of cool drinks to the waiting crowd. "Who was he, how did he die, is it okay for us to be here, to stand here?" I asked.

She responded, "A young Sherpa, cousin of my friend. He died instantly in a motorcycle accident on Kathmandu's crowded roads. Buddhists believe that the soul remains with the body until the funeral, so he is still with us."

Without warning, the chanting of funeral prayers ceased and we turned to watch as the mound of prayer scarves was removed, revealing a slender body wrapped carefully in white cloth. Male relatives lifted the body onto the funeral pyre, placing it correctly but gently in a cradle of logs of pine and fir, immediately covering the body with slender, fragrant green branches. Lighted torches were carried ceremonially around the pyre and then at a silent signal, bright flames were coaxed from the base of the pyre. They could not look at the mother, silent and withdrawn in her grief, her hands covering her face as her only son's soul departed, carried by the wind and smoke. "There is no social security in Nepal, he would have been their hope for comfort and care in old age."

Gradually the young crowd dispersed; their childhood friend had left them. Those who had to tend the fire remained. We returned silently to our taxi and our hotel.

Dolphin Story

I WOKE UP; it was a gorgeous sunny summer day. I hopped on my beach cruiser and headed to the beach. Wearing my triathlon wetsuit halfway on, halfway hanging off, I peddled in the warm morning air over the bridge, across the shallow waterway to the beach. It was a glorious day; there wasn't the tiniest bit of wind on the water. A head high south swell rolled in and closed out with a huge crash in the shallow water.

At any other time in the last 15 years, there would be one more piece to this equation – a surfboard in my hand. However, since throwing my back out two weeks before, I had taken up ocean swimming as a means of exercising and healing my body. Nevertheless, I couldn't help but think how nice the waves must have been at some of the better beach breaks.

As I approached the ocean, I noticed the waters were almost empty. This was very strange for such a beautiful day. Three lifeguard and sheriff boats patrolled the coast, something I had never seen before. It suddenly dawned on me – they must all be on the lookout for the 17-foot Great White shark that was spotted just three miles off Venice Beach the day before. I decided to go for my swim anyway. I wanted to use a new trick I learned from my friend Barbara, a world-class long distance swimmer, who had spent her life swimming in the open ocean. She shared with me that when her mind drifted to sharks as mine did this morning, she just repeated, "dolphin, dolphin," over and over in her head. "Dolphins have been known in the wild to scare off sharks," she explained.

Of course this technique is just to keep her mind occupied, I thought. It was a solid first step, though. Putting on my goggles, I dove into the clear water and began my one-hour swim down the coast. Images of a 17-foot shark swimming up under me filled my head. "Dolphin...dolphin..." I repeated over and over. As I approached the Venice pier halfway into my swim, I noticed a lifeguard boat hovering around the pier. Hmm...I had never seen that before. I scanned the horizon – no fins. The lifeguard wasn't yelling or waving his hands at me, so I figured I was safe.

I made my turn and headed back up the coast, against the current this time. That beautiful south swell looked so good until I was swimming against it. "Dolphin, dolphin, dolphin," I continued to repeat in my head. Before I knew it, I was at the end of my swim. I turned toward the beach and stopped to chat with a couple of surfers who were still out in the water.

"Hey, that was really cool!" one of them said to me.

"He probably doesn't even know," his buddy said.

"What don't I know?" I asked nervously.

"It was like five feet behind you the whole time. I have never seen that before!" he blurted with excitement. "You had a dolphin right behind you, following you, man. He was with you most of the way back!"

Somehow I had called in my own personal escort. "Dolphin, dolphin, dolphin." My new favorite mantra.

Paddling From Cuba –
Intuition & Action

O N JUNE 22, 2012, I landed in Havana, Cuba as part of a small kayaking team chosen to support professional long-distance swimmer Penny Palfrey as she attempted to set a new world record by swimming over 100 miles of open ocean from Cuba to the U.S. Unpredictable weather, shifting ocean currents and curious sharks were just some of the potential challenges that lay ahead. Having previously completed a 14-hour swim with Penny, I thought to myself, *How did I get here?*

It all started during a meditation three years ago. In the final month of my Master's Degree Program in Spiritual Psychology, I was in class quieting my mind when a crystal clear thought popped into my head: *I want to work with extreme athletes.* I opened my eyes, startled by the strength of the message.

I knew to pay attention to these kinds of signs. I wrote it down in my journal and set a strong intention. Two weeks later, my intention came to fruition. Eric, a friend of a friend, needed kayak support on his overnight swim to Catalina Island. Twelve plus hours of swimming non-stop without a wetsuit – sounded like an extreme athlete to me! I was in! Eric completed his swim and I found a new hobby and made a lifelong friend. As it turned out, the long-distance swimming community is pretty tight knit, so I soon found myself kayaking through the ocean with one of the best long-distance swimmers in the world: Penny.

During this extraordinary swim, Penny stayed very present and focused on the crew and what they were doing to help her with her swim. My kayak was right next to her towing the electric shark shield, and when Penny would come up for air, she would look right at me. Now normally, when you are kayaking, you are looking straight ahead, but when she would look at me, I would look right at her, smile and send her blessings and loving support. In my mind I imagined her as strong, healthy and completing her journey. She began to smile every time she would come up for air. It was enough for the other people in the support boat to notice. They asked me, "How come she is smiling? What's going on?"

Penny broke the world record for the longest unassisted long distance ocean swim – a record of 41 hours in the water before she had to be pulled out on July 1 due to a strong southeast current that made it impossible for her to continue her swim. The swim started on June 29 and ended July 1.

This was a journey of epic proportions - one that made history. My support role in this came as a result of what I learned at the University of Santa Monica (USM) - pay attention to the gentle whispers of my heart and be willing to be of service in my life, in ways both large and small. It was a total joy to be of service to this courageous woman.

The Power of Presence

In rivers, the water that you touch is the last of what has passed and the first of that which comes; so with present time.
— **Leonardo da Vinci**

ONE MORNING, I PADDLED INTO THE WAVES on my surfboard. Out on the water, old worries started taking over my thoughts. Trapped in my head, I felt separated from my body. I was doing my favorite thing, at my favorite surf break, with one of my favorite people, my brother. But it wasn't enough. I lowered my head down to my board and dipped my chin into the water. *Just be present to the moment,* I told myself. The cool water rose up to my nose and I could see tiny micro drops of water dancing above the undulating cool green surface. I imagined a whole world of tiny little creatures living happily in the waves in an incredible celebration of life. Time slowed down and my worries faded into the moment's amusement. I was no longer trapped in the past or worrying about the future. I was just completely in the moment. And for a short time, in the midst of a very challenging chapter of my life, I felt alive and free.

Intuition Experiment in Nepal

ON AN EXPLORATORY TRIP TO NEPAL several years ago, I found myself alone in the lakeside town of Pokhara. Much had changed since my first visit nine years earlier. The streets were full of coffee shops, Internet cafes and two-story hotels. This was a very different scene from the almost barren windswept town I visited in 2002; the new town was bustling with energy.

I had been in Nepal for three weeks now and had not yet decided which trail I wanted to trek. I was feeling frustrated and very alone. After a very brief internal pity party, I decided to turn things around with a little intuition experiment.

I am going to walk down the street slowly and consciously, I thought. I will use my intuition to guide me. When I get a sign, I will turn into a shop or restaurant and there will be my travel partner. With full confidence, (much to my amazement at the time), I walked silently down the long street, peeking into stores and coffee shops wondering whom I would travel with in Nepal. I was nearing the end of the street when I felt the gentle tug of intuition, a non-verbal but very clear "turn here." No way! I laughed to myself. Excited, but keeping my composure, I stepped into the restaurant and it was empty! My heart sunk. It didn't work, I thought. I turned to leave and then I heard the gentle clacking of a keyboard. Peeking around a straw partition, there she was, staring into her laptop absorbed by her work.

Mustering my courage, I walked over and asked the only thing I could think of. "How's the Internet here?" (*So lame,* I thought.)

She looked up with a smile. "Yeah, it's great, especially in this corner." There was only one table, the one she was sitting at.

"Can I sit with you?" She nodded yes. I put my computer back to back with hers and we started to talk. It turned out she was a professional athlete working for The North Face. Having just come off an expedition, she came to Nepal to relax. Who comes to one of the trekking meccas of the world to relax? Professional athletes do, apparently.

We ended up hitting it off, and 24 hours later, I was on the trail to the 13,500-foot Annapurna Base Camp with my new travel partner. Just as we started hiking, she turned to me and said, "There is one thing you need to know. I'm not waiting for you. I hike alone." I liked this girl already. She was the first person I had ever hiked with who consistently left me in the dust, day after day. I was impressed.

Each day we hiked at our own pace, sometimes bumping into each other, but always ending up at our final destination in the evening to share a steaming pot of hot chocolate and rum, watch the sun go down over the mountains and swap stories from the day. Every now and then I bump into Kasha and she is still skiing the mountains of the world, living the dream, a free spirit, waiting for no one.

Silence

*Most of the time we don't know what the hell is going on.
You could even be in a relationship or a career for 15 years and
not really know what is happening. All we need is one threshold
experience to open us up to what we are about and what it is
that we are actually doing here. And you might be emboldened
by it or horrified by it. And it's one of the reasons that we will
often not stop, and allow silence into our life...we know that our
surface personality will not survive the encounter.*
— **David Whyte, English poet**

ONE OF THE HARDEST THINGS for people to do, especially in our modern, fast-paced society, is to be silent. In all of my retreats, I include silence as a practice. I ask my participants to spend time walking alone through a village or along a trail, without talking. "Watch as your senses come alive," I tell them. "Watch as you slip into the role of the observer. Now observe your thoughts as they roll through your head. Walk slowly and methodically. Breathe slowly and just listen."

I find that silence can be one of our most profound teachers.

This is an email I received from a participant on a Nepal retreat. It is shared here with her permission.

"As I walked silently through the fog, deep in the Himalayas, alone on the trail, my deepest sadness came to me. The deep emotions of being raped as a young woman overcame me. Tears flooded down my face; I was alone, yet I felt surrounded by love. Love from my other trekkers who I knew were nearby. Love from myself, for knowing that I had chosen to go on this trip to heal. To move from a place of sadness to one of action and lightness. When I arrived at our camp spot, I felt light and free. The silence had set me free." — Shannon

The Square Grouper

I N MY EARLY 20'S I WAS INVITED to go on a last minute fishing trip in the Bahamas. I was sitting in the Miami airport on a four-hour layover when I got the call. It sounded so enticing, I canceled my flight home and within three hours I was speeding away from the Florida Keys on a fishing boat with my new friend Matt, his dad and Tim, his dad's buddy. Several hours out in the middle of the ocean, someone spotted a "Square Grouper" floating in the water. We pulled the large brown box into the boat and everyone was going crazy. "What's a Square Grouper?" I asked.

"Look!"

They cut it open and inside were what we later calculated to be several million dollars of cocaine, individually packaged and compressed into bricks. When I realized what it was, a chill ran through my body and my legs went numb. Immediately, I had images of newspaper articles with photos of dead tourists on the cover. My face was one of them. Looking around, nobody seemed to share my concern. As they pulled apart the packaging, I snapped pictures of everything. If we were killed, maybe the coastguard would find my waterproof camera floating in the ocean and my parents would know what happened to us. (I still have the photos.)

As the group was scheming about how they could sell the cocaine and what we could do with it, I saw a boat in the distance. "Look!" I shouted. I knew that drug drops had GPS locators in them and I thought that we had been discovered. My new friend's dad pulled out a stainless steel shotgun and held it below the edge of the boat. In a rush, I threw the package back into the water. We motored away from it and within a minute, a high-speed cigarette boat with three Cuban looking guys pulled up right next to us. We flashed our biggest, happy naïve touristy smiles, waved and showed them our fish. My friend's father was still holding the shotgun below the railing. The boat slowed down and the occupants checked us out and kept going, without a word. Whoa...that was close! The "Square Grouper" had floated away and was nowhere to be seen.

Later that afternoon, we arrived at our destination, a small island in the Bahamas. When we pulled up, Matt's dad was telling everyone, "You'll never guess what we found...blah blah." The harbormaster, a longtime friend of his, walked over and gave him an intense look that said, "it's probably not best to talk about this," and then walked away. An hour later, we checked into our beach house and the guys started pulling out huge chunks of compressed coke that they had cut out of the case before I tossed it. Matt, his dad the doctor and Tim, the young millionaire start-up guru, all started doing lines. Having never done it and always up for trying something new, I did a couple too. We were as high as kites.

After dinner we went out to a nightclub and Matt started bragging to a large group of cute girls that we had coke at our place and told everyone the story. I was on the way down from my high and I was starting to feel very nervous. This huge African American guy started talking to us and being really nice. He invited himself over with the girls. He seemed too eager, too nice, and I didn't trust him. In my gut, I knew there was something wrong, so I told Matt that I would run ahead of the group and clean our place up. I sprinted back and smashed all of the bags of coke flat, hiding them under a record collection. When the group arrived, Matt couldn't find the coke. He was really drunk and high and started getting really frustrated. I started whispering in people's ears that he was lying and that we really didn't have any drugs. People started getting nervous and the girls all bailed out. The only person who stayed was the buff African American guy. He egged me on, "Come on, I know you have it, come on, lets have some." I stuck to my story and asked him to leave. The party ended as quickly as it started. Soon everyone was asleep. Everyone but me.

It was 2AM now and I was lying on the couch in the living room. My heart was racing, and I had fallen so far from my high that I felt disgusted with myself. I wrote in my journal, "Today I am embarrassed to be me." I was now feeling really paranoid and every little noise sent me whirling around to see who was there. Suddenly, there was a knocking on the floor-to-ceiling glass window right next to my head. I jumped up to see the African American guy looking through the window, inches from my face. "Hey man, I know you have the coke, let's party!" he whispered to me enthusiastically though the glass, flashing a big Hollywood smile.

"I don't have anything," I explained. He didn't believe me. "Leave, now, or I'll call the cops!" I walked over to the phone and pretended to dial. He was gone. I ran into the bedroom and woke up Matt's dad and Tim to tell them what was happening. Tim looked at me with disgust.

"You rookie, it's the coke, you're just paranoid, go to bed!" I was fuming with rejection. I so looked up to this guy; I really wanted him to like me.

It was 3:30AM now and my still unnamed wannabe drug smuggling partner was back at my window. This time he wasn't smiling. "I know you have the coke, everyone knows, I'll help you get it off the island, my rate is fifty percent. I'll take half for the use of my boat. You get to keep the other half."

"I don't have anything!!" I whispered though the window. I wondered – if he really wanted it, why not just break the window and take it? He was twice the size of anyone in our group.

"Ok then, you are screwed, I tried to help you," he said. "The island police will be at your place by 6AM to raid your house." He left. Seconds later, I heard the sound of a handheld radio outside below the deck. My mind was racing. Was this real? If I tossed out the many thousands of dollars of coke and I was wrong, I would look like the biggest jerk. But if I was right, and I didn't get rid of it now, then we could all end up in jail. There was also a third option. What if I snuck out the back of the building and swam underwater to the sailboat anchored 100 feet from the shore and hid in the dingy?

I'll let these guys fend for themselves if they don't believe me, I thought. No, I can't do that, I can't just leave them. Screw it. I'll take my chances. I ran around the house, collecting the baggies of coke, wiped off the counters and the table and flushed tens of thousands of dollars worth of coke down the toilet. It was 4:30AM.

5AM. There was pounding on the door, and two men in military uniforms and two in street clothes, all armed with guns, were standing outside holding up a wrinkled piece of paper. "Open the door, we have a warrant." I ran to the bedroom.

"The police are here!" Everyone scrambled to wipe the last bits of coke off the counter tops in the bathroom.

"Open the door now, or we will come in on our own!" Before I was able to explain to the rest of the group what happened, the soldiers came in. With guns pointed at our chests, they sat us down, explained that we were being searched for possession of illegal narcotics and began to tear the house apart. Nobody talked. Everyone was scared white. I was the only one who knew the coke had been disposed of. I was feeling smug. They, meanwhile, were sweating and paranoid, shooting glances at each other wondering why I was so calm.

"Oh! Looks like we have something here!" The energy in the room took a huge leap. "What is this mon!?" one of the soldiers asked, looking at Tim. It came from his bag.

"It's just a little weed. It's a medical thing."

"Marijuana is illegal in the Bahamas, mon!" Tim was starting to shake. He reminded me of the guys who picked on me when I was a child. In that moment, I enjoyed watching him tremble. All of his power and clout was worthless in this moment. The thought circled around my head, *Who's the rookie now, Tim?*

The lead soldier asked him, "Do you have somewhere to be tomorrow or next week or next month?" Tim pleaded that he had to go home to be with his kids.

"Really? You have kids? I have kids too, mon. You lucky chance." The soldier was messing with Tim now, but this cruel joke was not funny, just like it wasn't for me in the hallway in 7th grade. The jokes weren't funny, they hurt. "Give me your wallet," he said to Tim. "You better have some picture of your kids, or you're not going home, mon." Tim pulled out the pictures. "Who's this?" It was a picture of a young girl.

"Pam." The soldier quickly whipped out another photo. "Who's this?"

"That's my son, Nick. His voice was trembling. The soldier stared at him then broke into a smile. "You lucky day, mon."

7AM. The soldiers got tired of tearing apart our rental house. They found nothing. Then, as if nothing had happened, their demeanor changed. They smiled, shook our hands and apologized for the inconvenience. They left the warrant on the table. We were told to pack up and leave for our own safety. Our boat had been pulled out of the water to be searched, but would be ready in a few hours, ready for us to leave. "Many people will be looking for the drugs, your story has gone around the island," they told us. While we waited for our boat at a local restaurant, a policeman stood outside the door. Sitting at our table, everyone joked about the whole thing. I was disgusted. Our boat was finally ready and we could leave.

On the way home everyone fished, told jokes and laughed about what a great story we were going to have. They bragged about how we got off clean (and I'll take full credit for that.) I just sat, feeling nauseous, playing back the whole experience in my head over and over. I thought about how many ways it could have all gone wrong and how we could have all been sitting in a prison in the Bahamas as our families got extorted for bail money. But it didn't go that way. I chose to follow my instinct every step of the way instead of bowing to social pressure.

Later in the week, I was on my flight back home. In the bathroom I had a thought. It was an addict's kind of thought. *They used my Swiss Army knife to cut all the coke open. I bet there is almost a line jammed in cracks.* This was pre-September 11, and my knife was in my pocket. I opened it up and tapped a small mound of powder onto the little plastic counter below the mirror. I felt my body respond. *Oh! I want that!* My response shocked me. I had only done it once and my body was already hooked. I looked up at the mirror and I looked myself straight in the eyes. *What are you doing?!* I wiped it up and for the second time that trip, flushed it down the toilet.

Lesson learned; Always follow your gut instincts. They may just keep you out of jail!

The Tuxedo Travelers

We can do no great things;
only small things with great love.
— **Mother Theresa**

I ONCE FOUND A WEB PAGE about two guys called the Tuxedo Travelers. They were two young English guys traveling around the world in tuxedos, doing stunts and gimmicks for money. On their web page, each stunt had a price attached to it and a PayPal® link. Once enough people donated, they would do a stunt, like drink warm snake blood, film it and post the video on their blog. It was all great fun, but they added another element that really caught my attention.

The money they raised was for charity, and it wasn't just donated to a cause. Instead, it was used immediately in their local surroundings. One of my favorite moments was when they acted out a ridiculous scene from a play in the middle of a bridge in Cambodia. After the performance, the travelers walked through the town gathering as many street kids as they could find and took them all out to a huge raucous meal at a local restaurant. It was a moment to remember for all involved.

Service, full engagement, inclusion and fun – that's what I learned from the Tuxedo Travelers.

Surrender Ten Miles to Tibet

People say that what we're all seeking is a meaning for life...I think that what we're really seeking is an experience of being alive, so that our life experiences on the purely physical plane will have resonance within our innermost being and reality, so that we can actually feel the rapture of being alive.
— **Joseph Campbell**

STANDING ON A THIN METAL SUSPENSION BRIDGE less than ten miles from Tibet, I can feel the warm wind on my face. Five hundred twenty-five feet below is the rushing Bhote Kosi River, fed by melted snow from the holy Mountain Kailash, the home of the Hindu god Shiva.

This is my last full day in Nepal. My mind is wandering. I could walk to Tibet in five hours. It's that close. I feel the pull. I went to Tibet seven years ago as a solo traveler, but now visitation is highly regulated by the Chinese Government and things have changed - for the worse. When I was there, local Tibetans pulled me aside on several occasions, closing their doors and windows to show me their scars from being beaten by the police and pictures of their beloved leader, the Dali Lama. They wanted to make sure we knew of their horrible oppression. It must have been wonderful to speak so openly to a stranger, knowing their thoughts and feelings were safe.

On the bridge, I am waiting. I'm not waiting to cross like the locals behind me. There are no mule trains in my way. I'm waiting to jump. Silently, I converse with my God. Not a specific God, but more of a universal, all-knowing, something-greater-than-me-ness. *The intention of my jump is to release fear, to let go of the addiction of control and to surrender.* I repeat this intention in my head over and over. A cameraman swings his lens into my face to record my pre-jump moments on video. "This is the beginning," I tell him. He speaks only a little English, and despite the intense look on my face, I can tell he does not understand.

I feel the fear in my legs. My new commitment to self has me terrified, not the jump. I was told there has never been a death here. However, today a part of me will die, gone forever; old ways of being released through a modern sky burial of the soul.

"Ninety-Four; Ninety-Four." I hear my number. "You jump now," he tells me. Ninety-Four; that's my weight in kilos. "Are you really ninety-four kilos?" the jumpmaster asks me three times in three different ways. I nod with a smile, trying to look confident as I wonder if maybe the scale is broken. "Very strong, big muscles," he says in an attempt to quiet his own disbelief. "He's just being thorough," I tell myself. "Surrender to the moment, trust the scale, trust the jump master, trust the cord and trust myself. I have done all I can; now it's time to let go of control.

Slowly, methodically, I walk my 94 kilos out to the edge of the steel platform. A tiny surge of adrenaline pumps through my veins and fills my heart with warmth. Smiling, I stand erect with my arms spread out in what Chris Cornell from Sound Garden calls the "Jesus Christ Pose."

"One...Two...Three." My feet leave the platform. Lightning, electrical synaptic ecstasy surges through my body, wind roaring past my ears like a jet engine, narrow green canyon walls blurred in my periphery; I'm falling through space, screaming out to the world a spontaneous proclamation, "I love you! I LOVE YOU! I LOVE YOU!!!"

Suddenly, something softly grabs my ankles and catches me before I hit the water. "No!! I'm not done!" I protest. My wish has been granted; I rebound and fall again. "Just one more moment, one last second..." Again I'm falling free. If this is what death feels like, I can't wait.

Hanging limp, slowly spinning over the river, I am alive. I have made the connection. The river has become the ceiling and the floor is the endless sky below me. Tibet looks beautiful upside down. Softly, I am lowered down to lie on a padded table while my safety gear is removed. I could lie here all day reveling in my joy, in the seconds of real time converted into a life experience.

With wobbly legs, I walk up the canyon trail, alone. The sun is warm on my skin and the air is silent. I wonder if I'm dreaming. Passing a tiny little mountain stream, I splash cold water on my face. No, I'm not dreaming. I feel radiant and intensely alive, floating six inches off the ground. I pass through a local village and smile at a farmer silently watching me. I feel like he knows how I'm feeling, like he's been there.

This is what I came for. This is why I came to Nepal. All of the days on my trip have led to this moment. I am no longer afraid. Fear to surrender to love... the path. The experience has been branded on my psyche, permanently. Anytime I have doubt, I know I can return to this moment for guidance...Trust, Courage, and Faith. All I have to do is leap.

All *you* have to do is leap...

Bring Nicaragua With You

S ITTING IN A COFFEE SHOP ONE DAY, in an ill-fated attempt to get "work" done, I somehow became a magnet for people in need of help. I was in a conversation with a friend about life coaching and suddenly someone leaned over to me. "Sorry to interrupt, but I heard you say you are a coach. When you are done talking, can I ask you a question?" I agreed and thus started my day with a string of people approaching me one after another. I caught their looks, I could feel them listening and mustering the courage to come over. I kept looking around the room, looking for the candid camera. I never did find it.

This is a story of a young man I met that day.

Logan was a 22-year-old surf instructor who shared with me about how he had come back from a year in South America and was having a hard time living in Los Angeles. This was noted by the fact that it was 2PM on a Tuesday and I could see his half empty bottle of Bacardi, not very well hidden behind his chair. "I miss waking up to the sound of the monkeys and eating mangoes for breakfast...the simple life. In Nicaragua, people ask, 'Who are you?' And it is usually followed by an invitation to talk or hang out. I can feel their genuine interest in getting to know me.

"Here," he continued. "Here, people just want to know what you do, so they can figure out if you can help them." Logan had been back six months and had started to create a new life in the

U.S., but his heart was clearly on the beach in his beloved Nicaragua. Feeling torn by the love he had for his woman living in the U.S. and the simple life on the beach, it appeared he had turned to daytime drinking.

This young guy had such a kind gentle heart, and I could see he was suffering. I began, "John, tell me more about Nicaragua...what is it you *feel* when you are there?"

"I feel free, alive. I feel open and loving. I feel connected to the people around me. I feel connected to t nature, the animals. Here I feel disconnected from all of that." Having lived abroad in Costa Rica, I could completely relate to what he was saying. I had been through the very same experience.

"John, what if what you are experiencing is just a test to get you to grow as a person?" I replied. "It's easy to hold that beautiful energy when you are immersed in it, but what about when you are not there?"

"When I'm in Nica, it's just natural," he said, with his eyes closed.

"Yes, it's easy and it's only the 1.0 version of being in the loving," I replied. He looked up at me, intrigued. "What if you could hold Nicaragua in *your heart*? What if you walk around in LA and *just be* that feeling you have in Nicaragua. What if you were the local representative of love, kindness, and openness? That is the 2.0 version of your experience. You want to walk with love in the world – it's time to graduate to holding that experience inside yourself no matter where you are." He put his hand on his heart and really felt into it.

"Yeah...I can do that." He smiled as he went on his way.

Life and Death on the Sea of Cortez

I get by with a little help from my friends.
— The Beatles

T 23 YEARS OLD, I was responsible for the entertainment, safety and ultimately the lives of 15 people on an 8-day kayaking trip in the sea of Cortez, in Mexico.

On the morning of the second day of the trip, the sea was glassy with not a ripple of wind. The sun was bright and the air was crisp. I had never seen the conditions so beautiful. We geared up all of the boats, packing our food and provisions for six days on the islands. Spirits were high and we were ready to go. Just as we started to put the boats in the water, Emilia, the wife of a local fisherman, ran down the beach to me. "Don't go out today Sr. Jesse. Please don't go out. The fishermen are all coming back from the ocean now. They say a big chubasco is coming." She was talking about northwesterly winds that whipped up out of nowhere and sometimes blew 60+ miles an hour. A chubasco could turn the glassy lake we had that day into a dangerous sea with overhead cresting waves.

"But the ocean looks perfect, Emilia," I challenged her. I could not see any of the usual signs. She held up her hand radio and I could hear the word chubasco being repeated over and over on the open channel. Looking back at the group, I could see the disappointment on their faces.

"Why aren't we going out? It looks fine." an annoyed client asked. I didn't respond. I just looked at Emilia. She was shaking her head at me. Having been stranded on the islands due to wind before, I knew what we were dealing with. We would stay put that day.

Unknown to me, at the same time, a mile down the beach, a group from UC Davis was also preparing to go out to sea. We would later learn that they too were warned to not go out. They ignored the warning.

The wind blew ferociously for 24 hours and by the next morning it stopped. The sea was again a lake, glassy and inviting. We awoke to the sound of a helicopter. Looking out over the sea, we could see a Mexican war ship had pulled into the bay, and search and rescue efforts were already underway. Several people from the UC Davis group were missing. Their boat had been capsized by a series of large waves. Several of the people on the boat were not wearing life jackets.

My assistant guide walked over to tell me that it was time for us to head home. "No, we are not," I argued. "Right now is the safest time ever to be in these waters. We are surrounded by search and rescue, the Mexican Navy and soon the media will be here swarming around. There is no way they are going to let anything happen to us." She was very shaken up, but I convinced her that this was a safe choice. I talked it over with the group and everyone agreed.

That day we paddled out on a perfectly flat ocean, without incident. As we neared our campsite, another group of kayakers paddled over to us. It was a second group from UC Davis. "Have you heard the news?" I asked the head guide.

"What news?" He didn't know! I paused for a second to think how I would lay this down gently.

Before I could compose my words a young guy named Nick blurted out, "Your other group, well most likely they are dead."

I shot him a glaring look. Nick was not known for his tact.

I explained what had happened and let them call home on our satellite phone. The newspapers were saying that UC students had died, but not specifically which group. They called home, assured everyone they were okay and headed back to land. We continued paddling and landed on Coronado Island. For the rest of the week the energy of the trip was split between the trauma of the tragedy that was still unfolding and our group trying to make the best our of our time together on that beautiful island.

We spearfished, hiked, swam and played. Occasionally a search boat would come by and pull us out of our little bubble and remind us of what was going on in the background. "Had we seen any floating bodies?" No. Every time I dove under the water, I wondered if there would be a pale, bloated body trapped in the kelp.

Caught in-between the space of tragedy and attempting to continue our adventure, an interesting thing happened. Every person on the trip except two people coupled up. By the end of the trip there were five new couples, one of which went on to get married. It seemed as though the intense energy surrounding the event had really brought people together.

When we arrived back on land, swarms of reporters and lawyers were waiting to interview us. They all wanted to know one thing: why had we heeded the warning? Why had we chosen to *not* go out?

The truth was, many guide companies come down and use the Sea of Cortez as a playground, but few take the time to make real relationships with the people that live there. Even though the weather report the day before did not show the coming chubasco, I deeply trusted the Daggett family and when Emilia says, "Don't go," I don't go.

Saved by a Stranger

MANY YEARS AGO, a very good friend of mine, Tammy, was in desperate need of a break from her nursing school studies. Her dream was to travel in Colombia. Finances were tight and she did not know if she could save enough money to go on the trip. She was determined to go, so she set a date several months out and set up her life to leave for a three-month trip to Central America.

A week before her departure time, she still did not have enough money to buy her plane ticket and was desperately trying to buy air miles off of someone or hoping that she could get a last minute cheap flight. Two nights before her trip she was in her apartment talking to her friend on the phone, telling him about her situation and feeling really desperate.

The next morning she woke up to go to work and taped to her door was an international round trip plane ticket voucher for American Airlines! Her neighbor, an airline attendant, whom she had never met, had heard her talking on the phone through the thin apartment walls and had reached out with a beautiful random act of kindness.

Two days later she stepped onto the plane bound for Colombia.

Live Like Dingo

A LUNG CANCER SURVIVOR with a huge scar right down the middle of his chest - the doctors had opened him up, cut out the cancer and put him back together. Humpty dumpty.

Mathew Wallace Smith was affectionately known as Dingo by friends and family. He touched so many lives with his simple generosity, kindness and almost uncanny ability to take any difficult situation and reduce it with a simple "no worries" or head nod, as if to say "these things happen."

A hard-working locksmith, he was on the path to "doing it right" in life: he had a stable career, a home and investments. Then one day he found out he had lung cancer and his world changed. After several years of treatment, he was finally declared cancer-free. Seizing his opportunity, Matt walked away from it all. He quit his career, sold his home, cashed his investments and took off to travel the world.

Working as a summer camp counselor, outdoor guide and educator between trips, he traveled for six months each year. Matt lived with such freedom, a freedom I had never experienced in another human being. He never said it, but I think there was a part of him that very well knew his cancer could come back, and he lived his life accordingly.

Matt's favorite way of going on adventures was to arrive in a country, find a hostel, drop off his bag and then jump on public transportation and go with no destination in mind. He often ended up in neighborhoods, slums and other areas where no tourist had ever been. There he would walk around, explore and meet people who were usually very friendly and open.

At the end of the day, he would pull out a card from his hostel and hand it to a taxi driver or bus driver. Even if he didn't speak the language, people could point him in the right direction and he eventually always made his way back home. Stepping outside all of the insulation that the well-worn tourist paths provide, Matt always went straight into being with the people. He had no fear, no hesitation – just a keen desire to explore and a natural ability to trust in the kindness of strangers.

Eventually, his cancer did return and he lived out his final days on a beautiful piece of land out in the Australian countryside.

Fish Soup and Humble Pie

I STUDIED ABROAD IN SEVILLE, SPAIN during my senior year of college. While living there, I contracted Hepatitis A from eating with a group of Spanish homeless people. They lived under an old stone bridge that happened to be not only a great place to sleep, but the best rock climbing spot in town. Every day after class, I headed down to the river to climb and we all knew each other on a first name basis. Even though they were living on the edge of society, I could tell that one of the ways my friends found dignity was in their meticulous preparation of food. Each day they begged for money, recycled bottles and went to market and purchased fresh vegetables and table wine. They even poured their wine into tall stemmed glasses; no drinking out of the bottle for this crew. After many day of refusing, I finally agreed to have some of their "famous" river fish soup. It was my first and last meal under the bridge.

I got so sick, I had to drop out of the program, return home and my partial credits did not transfer. My energy was extremely low and I had to make up an entire semester my last four months of college. When I graduated, I had no job, no internship and no plan. My girlfriend had gone back to her previous boyfriend while I was out of the country and I had to move back in with my parents. Needless to say, this was not what I had imagined my life would look like after college.

I quickly slipped into a depression. At the time, I wasn't even aware of this since I actually didn't believe that I was capable of being depressed. At 21 I still thought I was invincible (with the exception of this little hepatitis thing of course!) I remember the weight of my body, the slowness of my movements. Sometimes I could barely talk. My bedroom had been given to my little brother and so I slept on a mat on the floor of my father's office. Physically and mentally I felt like an old man whose life had passed him by. Everyone had big expectations for me, and there I was sleeping on the floor of my parents' house, unemployed, sick and depressed.

After a summer of doing very little, I pulled myself together and decided that I had to do something. I ate a huge piece of humble pie and went back to a summer job I had four years earlier, working as a stockperson in a warehouse. Everyone I worked with was still there. "What are you doing back here?" they asked. "I thought you went to college?" I was deeply ashamed, though I tried not to let it show. I didn't even have a car, having rented it out for the year for extra money. Every day, my father was kind enough to drop me off and pick me up from work. I tried to focus on being grateful, but really I just felt like I had completely failed myself and my family.

One morning I woke up and asked myself, if I could do anything, what would I do? Motivational speaker and coach came into my head. *That's not going to happen for a while,* I thought. *My life is anything but inspiring.* Then I asked, *what would #2 be?* Acting popped into my head. I felt an immediate rush. In that moment I committed to giving it my best shot. After two months, I was accepted into an acting program, and I had saved enough money working in the warehouse to pay for the first two semesters. It was time for me to leave. I went to tell my boss, a spry little Filipino lady who would most likely spend the rest of her life working in the warehouse along with the rest of her family.

Looking me squarely in the eye, she said to me, "I don't ever want to see you here again." She smiled, gave me hug and shooed me out the door.

HEALING

As a coach, a major focus of the work I do with people is around pursuing exciting goals. At the same time, I have experienced that the most powerful work we can do to move ourselves into greater ways of being happens on the inside. The changes we make on the inside profoundly affect the world around us. And the best part is, when we heal our unresolved issues, our personal gains are ours to keep forever. Nobody can take them away from us.

> *Outer experience is a reflection of inner reality.*
> **— Dr.'s Ron & Mary Hulnick**

Nothing to It, but to Do It

Sometimes you just have to take the leap
and build your wings on the way down.
— **Kobi Yamada, Author and publisher**

WHILE ORGANIZING A RETREAT TO GUATEMALA, my friend said to me, "You must meet this friend of mine. He does healing meditations with gongs and Breathwork." This sounded a bit weird, but I was open to it.

At her home, lying on the floor in a circle, with eyes closed, we began to breathe. Five minutes into the session, my whole body started to buzz with energy; I could feel stress and fear leaving my body. Images of a new adventure for my retreat business flooded into my head. I stopped breathing and blurted, "Hand me a paper and pencil, I want to get this all down before I forget it." I had not felt this energized in months.

I started the breathing sequence again, and for the next thirty minutes, I experienced deep states of bliss, calm and connection to myself.

Before the session was over, I knew I wanted to learn this technique. "Where did you learn this?" I asked.

The healer replied, "As a matter of fact, the next healer training starts this weekend!" There were two spaces open, and the training ended the day before I was scheduled to leave for Peru.

Serendipity at its finest. I signed up immediately and immersed myself in the program.

On Monday, I stepped onto a plane to Peru. As soon as I arrived, I posted a flyer at my hotel. It read, "Breathwork Meditation Session with Life Coach Jesse Gros." Still riding off the high from the weekend, I wanted to use my new skills immediately.

That evening, I set up the circular room with candles, mats and blankets and burned some Palo Santo (a Peruvian aromatic wood used in ceremonies). I sat cross-legged with meditation music playing in the background, feeling somewhere between some kind of a spiritual teacher wannabe and just hoping somebody would show. I waited, trying to look natural. Sitting cross-legged is very painful for me, so I ended up just sitting on my feet and letting my legs go numb. It's not easy what we do.

One by one, they walked in to the room. The first was a woman in her mid fifties who I recognized as a visiting group leader of a spiritual retreat that was due to arrive soon. *Surely I had nothing for her,* I thought. She smiled and asked if she could lead a prayer as part of our session together. Jealousy and insecurity pulsed through me. "Of course," I responded, smiling with a big, forced grin. Next came a couple; I quickly recognized the young man as a big professional mountain skier from the U.S. Great...now I had a professional healer and a celebrity athlete. Gulp. A few other people trickled in, and to my joy, they all seemed to be just regular folks. That is, with one exception: the woman who managed the retreat center, surely a veteran of healing work, showed up at the last minute, adding to the celebrity roster.

Feeling nervous and a bit shy, I started with a simple introduction, straying far away from sounding anything like an expert. "Hi. I'm Jesse; I'm a life coach. Today I'm going to share with you one of the most powerful tools for healing and relaxation I have ever been exposed to." After my intro, the trip leader woman launched into a full speech with vim and vigor, walking around the room and speaking with a commanding tone. One by one, she did what I can only describe as "knighted" each participant as a member of a group of spiritual brothers and sisters I had never heard of. I felt like my session was being hijacked! I just sat and watched each person's expression in the room, trying to get a sense if anyone felt as uncomfortable as I was. To my surprise, everyone looked perfectly content and nobody left the room. After what felt like hours, she was finished and it was my turn.

I dimmed the lights, started the music and began. Soon the entire room was breathing together and we began the process of moving into a deep meditative state. People breathed, wiggled and adjusted, and a young woman opened her eyes and looked over at me. *Oh no! I must be doing something wrong,* I thought. She just smiled and closed her eyes. Maybe she was just checking in.

"You may experience some resistance to the process. Just keep breathing," I shared. Twenty minutes went by, and then it happened: the retreat leader started to gently sob. *Here we go,* I thought. "You may experience some emotions coming to the surface, and that's okay... just let them bubble up," I offered. One by one, each person started to open up in their own way. Some gently cried, some shook and others laughed out loud. "If there is anything you have been holding onto, just let it go," I guided. The energy of the room jumped.

I moved from person to person, assisting them when I could feel they were stuck. "If it's not Love, it's not yours. Just breathe through it," I offered. As the energy of the room elevated, people went deeper and deeper into their experiences. With some, I could feel exactly what they were moving through - the personal material that was creating upset for them. I never asked, but somehow just knew.

After we completed our sharing circle at the end of the session, the trip leader, the retreat manager and the athlete all shared that they had had profound experiences. "How long have you been doing this?" they asked. I had hoped nobody would ask me this.

"It's my first time," I confessed.

I continued to lead Breathwork sessions and six months later, I found myself at a huge coaching conference in Arizona. I signed on as a participant, but I knew inside that I would be teaching. Upon arrival, I learned that there were a few small rooms available for participants to guest teach on a very limited basis. I wrote up a simple paper sign-up list and put it on the conference board.

The first morning, six people showed up to breathe. They loved it! At the end of the session, several people asked me if I would lead another. "Sure, but I don't have a room. All of the rooms are booked for event speakers," I replied.

"Listen," a young feisty coach from Chicago said. "You agree to lead it, and I'll find you a space!"

An hour later, I had a room and the handmade sign-up sheet went up again. This time, twelve people showed up. Things were going great. The request came for another session and then another. It was starting to take on a life of its own. When the sign-up sheet was full, someone added an additional page and it filled as well. I started getting worried that the event coordinators would pull the plug, since I wasn't on the official roster as a presenter. I was no longer under the radar. I needed a bigger room.

I was approached by one of the event directors. "You can call off the dogs," she said. "We will get you rooms. Just tell me what you need." It turns out my little advocate from Chicago was really hustling on my behalf.

"Well... actually, I would like to have the main ballroom tomorrow morning." I could feel my face getting red. Surely I had gone too far.

"Let me get back to you," she said.

I know what that means, I thought. *Don't let her go.* "Ok, I'll wait right here. Take as long as you need," I said. I could see her irritation. She knew we were not going to give up.

"I'll give you the ballroom on one condition. You have to be out of there by 9AM and it can't look like anyone has been there."

The final morning, I led a session in the main ballroom for over fifty people. People loved my sessions and the requests kept coming in. Could I lead a session for this group and that leadership team? I led sessions into the wee hours of the night and the next morning, up until the last moment when I had to leave for the airport. I was exhausted, but buzzing with energy from being able to make such a huge contribution.

The most beautiful moment of the weekend occurred when a young woman who had recently lost a child shared that she had connected to her unborn baby while she was deep in the meditation. As she shared, tears streamed down her face; she was glowing with joy and the entire room was spellbound. She shared, "My little girl wanted me to know that she's happy and that everything is going to be okay."

All in all, I ended up working with a third of the entire conference. My simple experiment had grown totally out of control, in the best way. "Nothing to it, but to do it," my father always told us.

Saying Goodbye to Rosebud

IN ORDER TO CREATE SPACE for new things to grow in our lives, we must first clear out anything that is in the way of us moving forward. Often simple things like holding onto old photos or letters can keep us energetically attached to an old relationship, for example. Another place where this energetic "stuckness" can show up is around incomplete projects, like the four different paintings we started and never finished, or the book we started to write and gave up on. It does not matter how big or small the project was; left incomplete, it sucks our motivation, leaving us trapped in energetic purgatory. Over the years, I have been shocked by how much emotional energy can be caught up in an object.

Have you ever had something you used to do a lot, and then just stopped? And then you tried to start it up again, only to notice some kind of invisible resistance? It seems unusually difficult to start up again and you find yourself reminiscing about how it used to feel or how much easier it used to be? Maybe your creativity just feels flat, or the resistance is so strong, you can't even get yourself to start up again.

It may be time to clean house, both literally and energetically.

A film producer friend of mine called me over one day to help him clean out his garage. Normally, this would not be my first choice of activities on a Saturday, but I knew his garage would be filled with all kinds of interesting entertainment history, so I agreed. After several hours of digging through old film projects, signed pictures from his years as an agent and framed movie deals scribbled on napkins, he asked me if I could help him out with one final box. "I want you to help me say goodbye to Rosebud. I can't do this alone."

He was ready to let go of his biggest incomplete project; a feature film that had consumed his life for eight years and nearly bankrupted him. Aside from the money and thousands of hours of work that had gone into his film, Steven was deeply connected to the lead character in the film. A young female revolutionary in the 90's, Rosebud had been killed by police in what amounted to a closed investigation based on what Steven and many others believed to be inconclusive evidence. He had suspicions about what really happened to Rosebud and this film was set to expose the people who had killed her.

On the eve of his film moving into full production, September 11th happened and his producer told him that this film could not be made because "America has no taste for revolutionaries right now. Were she alive now, Rosebud would likely be on a domestic terror watch list." Crushed, Steven abandoned the project.

Years later, with the successful documentary *FLOW* under his belt, we stood outside Steven's now almost empty garage. One final box from Rosebud remained in the center, on the cement floor. We all shared parting words, lit a single candle, turned off the light and left Steven to be alone in the garage with Rosebud. It was a very personal and deeply respectful way to say goodbye to a project that he had poured so much of his heart and soul into. As we waited outside, I was reminded just how far as a society we have moved away from our traditional ways of ritual and honoring our efforts. The door opened, and he handed us the box knowing he would never see it again. The Rosebud chapter was now closed.

Steven shared with us over the weeks following how he could feel the weight of sadness and failure lift. He experienced a creative resurgence, which is just what he was looking for.

And the Truth Will Set
(Your Creativity) Free

DURING A SHARING EXERCISE at a motivational seminar, a woman sitting next to me shared that she had been deeply hurt by her husband's flirtatious behavior with other women early in their marriage. She explained that he would sometimes come home late at night after work with lipstick on his collar. He denied any wrongdoing and she believed him, but she never felt truly resolved. Her upset silently festered for years. It was something she had never really spoken about with anyone. I listened deeply and she felt that she had really been heard.

A month later, I asked her if she had gotten anything out of the seminar. She said that a lot of it was familiar information and actually there were parts of the weekend that she really didn't like. However, she said, "The most interesting thing has happened! Before the seminar, I had resistance to doing my choreography work. Now all of the sudden, new ideas are just flowing out of me. I'm back in the studio. I'm so excited!"

I have shared this simple story with many people, because this woman's work is very prolific and touches many people in powerful ways. I also find it to be one of my favorite stories to share, because I just love how simply sharing our truth with others and feeling heard can lead to healing that opens us up in the most unexpected ways.

The Shame Takes Up All the Space

THE RAIN HAD STOPPED and I was lying in the garden of a Peruvian shaman. The sun was peering through small gaps in the clouds, illuminating the flowers and warming my shivering body. I was just coming out of a very intense and enlightening ceremony, one that I would later see as one of the more profound spiritual experiences of my life. Wiping the tears from my face and smiling at the beauty of the garden, Dieter, a German engineer and a participant in our group, walked over to me and shared the following. "I have a message that I feel I have to share with you. I have no idea why. It just popped into my head." He hesitated and stared at me for a moment. I could see him straining to speak. "The shame takes up all the space," he said.

My body shook as his words landed. My heart opened suddenly, and I could feel all of the sadness on the planet. I had tapped into a deep well of grief inside me that I didn't even know existed. I could feel the trees, the rivers, the animals. I felt shame for the way we have treated our precious planet, for the way I had just been on the take from Mother Earth my whole life, sucking on her tit like a 38-year-old fat baby that never grew up. What had I given back? I used the water, the land, the plants, the air, the minerals and the animals. I used all of it to sustain me. I had gobbled down food most of my life and never had really been thankful for what it provided for me. I never stopped to pay homage to the animals that were slaughtered to provide me with meat. I never appreciated the water that flowed instantly from the faucets in my house.

It was a sadness that left me feeling like a parasite, like part of a species destined to extinguish itself with greed and disconnection from the source of its own life. And there I was, just living my life, carving out my little niche like an ant in an ant farm, waiting for the day when someone would shake it up and destroy all I had worked for. I had a career, a home, accomplishments and beautiful pictures on Facebook. And all for what?

No matter what I accomplished in the material realm, I realized that I had to rectify this deep feeling of betrayal against the planet, and ultimately of myself, if I was to ever be deeply happy. I had to clear this shame if I was ever to move beyond my own cynicism about the future of the planet and our species.

I started with gratitude.

Gratitude for all that I receive from the earth on a daily basis.

I moved into respect.

Respect for myself, for knowing that I could make a difference in my lifetime.

I moved into action.

I committed to reducing my waste by half.

The next morning, I woke up with an amazing gift.

I woke up with one beautiful, simple and profound thought in my mind:

There is no shame.

I repeated this to myself over and over.

There is no shame.

Like a new suit, I tried it on.

What if there was no shame? How would I be? Who would I be?

I would be Peaceful.

I would be Compassionate.

I would be free from my bondage of cynicism.

Free to make a difference.

All day, I repeated, *there is no shame.*

And my heart filled with love and possibility.

And I felt like my young, optimistic self once again, twenty years later.

I Don't Trust God

FTER A FREEZING COLD MORNING of surfing in Malibu, I was happy to be inside, sitting in my chair. For two days in a row, I had gotten up at 5AM to take Dustin, a fellow graduate student, surfing. Two days before, he had stood up in front of our class of 200 people and shared that it was his dream to learn how to surf. Could anyone take him out? His request was simple yet somehow profoundly vulnerable. I stood up. "I'll take you." The days were long. We were in class from 9AM until late in the evening. Adding a morning surf session was a real stretch.

This morning I was exhausted physically, mentally and emotionally. The nature of our psychology Masters program was that we worked on our own personal issues in class. Today, I didn't want to face my life. I just wanted to escape. As our class started, I was already falling asleep in my chair. After a short lesson, our professor requested that we turn our chairs to form groups of three. First I was the counselor, then the observer and finally it was my turn to sit in the client's chair. Every part of me wanted to run. The instruction was to talk about a time recently when we had felt unsafe. *Right now, sitting in this chair*, I thought.

I started off by sharing to my classmate counselor, "I really don't want to be here. I am so exhausted." She smiled and encouraged me to share. My defenses were so low, I couldn't argue and started sharing. I couldn't think of a specific story, so I started generally. "It's very hard for me to trust people. Especially men," I shared.

"Tell me more," she said.

"I really don't want to share, but here goes anyway. I got ruthlessly bullied as a child, mostly by older boys. They were cunning and tricky. I learned to not trust."

"Tell me more," she said.

My energy was dropping and my head hung low. I continued to share. "I don't know what else to say...this mistrust, it's just in me." There was a long pause and then she leaned into me and gently said, "Do you trust God?"

"What?"

"Do you trust God?" she asked again with a gentle smile. I had never been asked that question, by myself or by anyone. An image flashed in my head. I was four years old. Sitting with my mom, I told her, "I don't believe in God."

My classmate counselor said, "It's okay, God looks different for everyone." I saw a vision of the universe – purple, blue and white dots of sorts. A hot flash moved through my body.

My eyes rolled up, and the answer I heard in my head was, "No. I guess I don't. I don't trust God." My whole body started to shake, my lips quivered. I struggled to hold it in.

"Would you like to?" She was looking at me like a little child.

"That feels really scary." I had always admired my friends who seemed to be truly connected to a higher power. Mormons, Buddhists, Christians, Spiritualists...they all seemed to have a level of peace and calm that I never felt. I had always been stopped by my distaste for organized religion and something deeper, something unnamed.

"Okay, I hear you...and would you be willing to try to trust, just a little?" Her voice was soothing.

"I don't know. I want to." My voice was trembling and my whole body was now shaking uncontrollably. I felt like a terrified young child standing on the edge of a high dive. She was the gentle voice saying, "Just put your toes on the edge." Tears streaming down my face, fluid gargling up my throat, I took a deep breath. "Okay...but just – just a test. But just for a week." More tears, fear. "I'm soooo scared." I took another deep breath, sitting up straight. I opened my mouth to speak and the words wouldn't come out. My voice just squeaked. No words. I could feel them trapped in my throat. Mustering every bit of will-power I had left, I closed my eyes and whispered the words. "I trust you."

And it all poured out. Years, maybe lifetimes of grief, disconnection and longing...I sobbed uncontrollably. My entire body pulsed up and down. I had lost control, something I had feared my whole life. There was only deep heaving, whole body sobs, tears, snot, and my voice was almost unrecognizable to me. When I finally pulled my head up, the classroom was almost empty, as everyone had gone to lunch. My classmates were sitting by my side. Over an hour had gone by. "Please don't leave me alone," I asked. For several hours I sat with an assistant, a blanket over my shoulders, buzzing with energy, feeling layers of mistrust peel away. I felt like I was walking two inches above the ground. I was so grateful for those morning surf sessions, which had exhausted me and lowered my defenses so much that my ego could no longer put up a fight. I could no longer resist the very thing I had always wanted and yet had no clue how to get.

God, Spirit, Mother Earth, the universe, the spaghetti monster...whatever you call it, well, he passed the test. We made it through the first week and our relationship has long moved past provisional trust status. I have also learned to trust myself and others at a level that I had never experienced before.

The Least Important Member
of the Family

WHEN I WORK WITH CLIENTS over the course of a year, they often bring me specific goals that they want to work on. I call this the outer journey. And in the process of moving forward towards their goals, we inevitably unearth the inner blocks that have been keeping them from getting the things they really want in life. I call this the inner journey. It's the place where most people have a blind spot and have the most potential for growth.

Rhonda's story:

Rhonda's goals starting out were business-related. Her main goal was to quit her job, go back to graduate school and get trained to be a therapist and a coach. She was very specific about what she wanted. While we moved towards her goals, it soon became clear that there was something going on underneath the surface for her that was blocking her progress. She knew what she wanted, but she felt totally blocked from taking action on her vision. (This was a very strange experience for a self-proclaimed workaholic who was accustomed to going after what she wanted.)

Over the course of several months of us working together, she realized that she'd been carrying around a feeling of fundamental unworthiness for much of her life. This stemmed from an underlying belief that she was the least important member of her family. She shared: "My recollections of my childhood were that my parents spent lots of time and energy on my sisters and their well-being and I just got lost in the shuffle. I was alone a lot and was always looking after myself."

This feeling was affecting her ability to pursue her dreams not only in her career, but in relationships, as well. This theme had been playing out in her life for years. In our work together, she was able to re-story the meanings about her earlier experiences to those based in truth instead of misinterpretations. The culmination of this work came when she was able to speak with her parents about their relationship. They were shocked to learn what she'd been telling herself for so many years; it couldn't have been farther from the truth!

She shared: "My identification as unworthy was totally unfounded! I just made it up! Since then, I feel like a different person. And, for the first time in almost 39 years, I am doing exactly what I want to be doing because I chose it. That feels amazing."

She ended up leaving her career, marrying her man and is now enrolled simultaneously in two psychology graduate programs.

An Early Experiment into the Nature of Love

WHEN I WAS A FRESHMAN IN COLLEGE, I went on an 8-day Wilderness Education Program backpack trip in the Sierras. During our trip, we had a 24-hour solo experience. Our leaders put each of us in our own area with set boundaries and left us there with no food, no clothes, a sleeping bag, sunscreen, two pencils and a notepad. We were not allowed to talk or to move out of our area. During the day I sketched in my book, wrote poems and wrote about life. The answers to many of my problems just seemed to show up, effortlessly. At night I tried to go to sleep, but because I couldn't talk, my thoughts became louder and louder, racing and pacing around in my head. I had dozens of reoccurring dreams and started to feel like maybe I was going a little crazy. It was a long night.

By morning, my thoughts started to quiet down and then all of the sudden they just stopped. My mind was empty. There were no voices, no thoughts, nothing! I just sat there for about half an hour and then my eyes started to water and I was swept up by the overwhelming beauty of my surroundings. In that moment I could hear every little sound around me. I put my head to the ground and I could even hear the ants moving in the dry soil. I was struck with an idea and decided to test it out. I wanted to know if the feeling of love I experienced was the result of something I *received* from somebody, like a gift, or if it was merely a reflection of the love I was giving.

I walked over to a large, red, peeling Madrone tree and gave it a huge hug. In my head I said, *I love you.* There I stood, in the middle of the forest, standing naked and sunburned, hugging a tree with tears in my eyes and I thought, *Damn, I hope nobody walks by.* I looked around and nobody was there and so I did it again, and there it was – I felt love from this tree! I was truly a tree hugger.

There was no need to conduct any further tests. I had drawn my conclusion.

The feeling of love is merely a projection of the love already inside you.

There is no need to go out searching for something that already lives inside.

The Most Dangerous Place
in the World

WRITTEN BY A CLIENT:

"The most dangerous place in the world is 'maybe,'" my coach says to me this morning. "Either say 'Hell, yes!' or a strong 'no,' then move on. A strong yes or no sends your energy in the right direction. All those maybes are like sucks - they just pull energy out of you and they're just constantly floating in your head."

We were talking about my book, and how this endeavor to write it has lingered around me as a major 'to do' since I embraced the idea that words were both my passion and career. I have a Word document that's always open, one which has chapters of my manuscript, but it just sits in the background of all the other things I do on my computer day in and day out, as this guilty and shameful reminder of what I feel like I 'should' be doing.

"Oh, you just need to throw that feeling away right now," he tells me, strongly. "Guilt is a worthless emotion. You can't shame yourself into achievement."

Instead, he encourages me to reflect on what it'd feel like to either shelve the project, say yes wholeheartedly, or a big emphatic no to the project. Surprisingly, I feel a bit of resentment towards the book and want to say "Hell, no."

"A strong no is worth 100 yeses," he encourages. "If you're meant to do it, you'll come back to it. But for now, what you're feeling is valuable. Let it be." The thing is, I've had opportunities to show my manuscript to editors and agents that other budding authors fight to have, chances that were handed to me, but I just wasn't ready to take advantage of them.

As I learned a while back, even if it's the right thing at the wrong time, it's still the wrong thing. "There's clean resistance to keep you out of harm's way," my coach imparts, "and then there's muddled resistance to keep you out of growth's way."

We both pause. That was a biggie. "Wow," he says to me. "I've always had that philosophy floating around, but this is the first time I've put it to words. I'm going to write that down." I did the same. And, once I said NO strongly, I was amazed at how free I felt, how liberated, how empowered. These two big things in my life - my eating disorder and my book – that I've held onto for security and comfort for almost two decades went *poof*, because I chose to make peace with them and let them go.

We chat a bit more in terms of figuring out what next steps I can take to move in a positive direction, even if they're super small. There's been a lot of emotional cleaning and clearing as of late, and so we talk about putting these files on an external hard drive and removing any reminders of the book from my apartment.

"I've learned that where you are right now," my coach offers, "is the time to pay attention to the quiet murmurs of what's drawing your attention. As a child, if you're not given a safe space to let the soft things run the world, knowing that you'd be taken care of and that you'd be okay, then you're not accustomed to that. To soften now, to let your guard down and let whimsical stuff show up is to say, 'Hey, I feel safe enough. The castle walls are defended enough. I can go do what I want and not have to look over my shoulder while doing it. I don't have to worry that someone's going to attack me.'"

I teach my yoga students all the time about feeling safe, about how I'm holding that sacred space for them to feel secure. And, with Jesse's words, I realize that I've cultivated that for myself too, even if it means letting go of who I thought I was and embracing who I continue to become.

What a triumphant, growing-up moment.

— Judy

Breaking the Illness Cycle

S TARTING AT 10 YEARS OLD UNTIL AGE 25, I had a major health challenge every 4 years. At 10, I fell headfirst off the roof of a building and had 70+ stitches in my head. I rode my bike home, with my head open, gushing blood.

At 14, I contracted viral and bacterial meningitis. My parents found me on the floor hallucinating and crawling around the living room.

At 18 my left lung collapsed. I was on my way up to the roof of my school's engineering building where I had set up a surprise Valentine's dinner for my girlfriend. I never made it to the top. Two weeks later, my lung collapsed a second time. My doctor labeled it a "spontaneous" event, meaning he didn't have a clue why it happened. I had lung surgery and was told I could never scuba dive or go to high altitudes.

At 21, I contracted Hepatitis A while studying abroad in Spain. My doctor said that my liver was so damaged by the disease that I could never drink again.

At 25, I got a horrible fungal infection in my leg while traveling in Mexico and the whole thing puffed up like a balloon. I should have known I was in trouble when my skin doctor excitedly called all of his colleges in to see. "I have never seen this before!" he exclaimed. My knee bothered me for two years and it looked like I might need surgery.

After that event, I started to check in and decided it was time to break this mysterious four-year cycle. I had a deep sense that these events were not just random. Looking back, up until then, I had been putting a lot of energy into directions of my life that were not in alignment. I worked like a dog to overcome my natural resistance to the way I was living and my body seemed to be paying the price. At 25 years old, I decided to drop out of my path to becoming a doctor.

I went to Bikram Yoga and practiced six days a week for four months. I healed my knee - no surgery needed! This began the process of slowing down and checking in with my body, of listening to my body and following its directives. Since then, more than once I have received clear messages that my lung collapse was an attempt by my body to slow me down. I got the same message from my liver. *Slow down.* During both incidents, I was running around like a maniac, creating an overly busy life and unable to enjoy my surroundings. I was deaf to the messages from my body, which was quietly trying to guide me away from danger and towards a healthier life.

On one occasion, I worked with an indigenous medicine doctor and during the session, I visualized a black cloud leaving my lung. I got a clear message that my lung was healed. Having tested my lung on several "lower" mountains, I was still hesitant to go to any real altitude. The next day, I climbed a 15,000-foot peak in Peru and my lung felt great! Years of fear and trepidation all washed away.

I also enjoy wine and craft beer, my liver levels are normal and my knee continues to function beautifully. All of the things I was told by my doctors did not come true. Let me be clear – I am very grateful for allopathic medicine for saving me from myself over the years. And, I feel that I have moved on and learned how to take care of myself by slowing down and allowing my body's wisdom to guide me.

It's been 14 years and I continue to be free of illness and injury.

An Emotional Sherpa

L EANING IN SO FAR EMOTIONALLY, I could feel her pain. I could feel where her lessons were lying, waiting to happen. "I can carry that weight for you. Let me carry that emotional weight. After all, I can handle it. I am strong." This was the beginning of many of my past relationships.

My friend, a therapist, calls this the Superman Syndrome. It refers to people who choose to be in relationships with people who they feel need to be "saved" or rescued. The superhero unconsciously chooses someone as a project, as a means to feel empowered and also as a way to avoid doing their own work, or focusing on their own growth.

For years, I had helped people in this way. Becoming enmeshed in other people's growth was my specialty, and doing so moved me into a form of low-level co-dependency. Only my version had a slight twist: "Don't worry about me, my feelings don't really matter, let's just get you taken care of." And on I trekked through life, carrying the emotional weight of those around me. I prided myself in my ability to not have many needs.

"How can you coach others though difficult challenges and not take on their challenges as your own?" a client of mine once asked. The truth is, in the past I did. Their wins and their defeats were my own. Up and down - it was exhausting. I knew when I was enmeshed, because after a session, I would be exhausted instead of empowered. "Let me carry that for you. Let me extend the helping hand of over-responsibility." The hand was disguised as noble work but the offer was built on the assumption that they could not do it themselves. This assumption, at its very core, dishonors the person being "helped" and secretly allows the "helper" to feel superior.

I have seen this in therapist friends of mine. Unable to separate themselves from the weight of their client's burden, they take it on, bit by bit, where it often shows up as physical weight. They are literally carrying the "weight" for their clients.

Are you an Emotional Sherpa? Walking around with a 150 lb bag lashed to your back, piled high with the troubles of those you love, walking almost barefoot in the snow, while those around you bounce along carrying nothing but the simplest bits? Are you proud of your work, yet exhausted by the people you serve?

I was.

To detach myself from this behavior, I found a mantra that has served me well:

"I am not responsible for other people's feelings."

"I am not responsible for other people's healing."

"I lead the way, I listen, I ask questions, I reflect."

In a dream, I am moving through the relationships of my life, revisiting each one. *Mom, I will no longer carry that burden for you. Theresa, I set you free,* and on it goes, through the female relationships of my life.

I no longer rescue people. No one is broken. Nobody needs fixing. I honor them by knowing that they have all of the inner resources they need to heal themselves and pursue their destinies.

Unexpected Healing in Peru

All knowledge is divided into three domains:
What we know, what we know that we don't know,
and what we don't know that we don't know.
— **Werner Erhard**

A S A COACH, my favorite realm of learning is in "What we don't know that we don't know." People often show up on retreat with lists of things they want to get out of the experience. The lists are full of things they know. The real fun happens when they walk away with an unexpected experience that is far more valuable than what they came for, something that they didn't even know to ask for.

As part of the application process for my retreats, I always ask that people leave space open for the unexpected or even a miracle.

During a retreat in Peru, one of my clients had a beautiful, unexpected experience. Briana came to Peru because she wanted more freedom to be herself. She wanted to be more present and spend much less time in her head. She was also ready to create space for a man in her life. During our journey, we hiked remote trails to Machu Picchu, volunteered in an indigenous village, joined in an ancient ceremony with local Shamans and expanded our vision of ourselves through a multi-day coaching process. After returning home, she sent me an email. This is what she shared:

Discovering the truth about me:

Going on this trip to Peru I had several intentions, one of which was to just be fully present to my experience and not think about home. I certainly did that - but I gained a lot more than I expected.

Since I was a small girl I had this quiet, underlying belief that somehow I was "bad" - a belief that kept me from getting close to people for fear that I would be "discovered." Mentally, I knew this was not true, but some part of me refused to let it go. I figured, I'm smart, I'm an engineer, I can figure this out. I couldn't.

During the trip, we did several breathing meditation sessions. During the first one I went to a dark place and cried it out unexpectedly - but after my cry I felt a weight had been lifted. I can't tell you what it was, but I felt like I was floating in the stars - I could see them in front of me. I could literally feel the healing take place.

Again, during the ceremony with the local Shaman, I found myself going to a challenging place. At first I was scared, but soon realized that this is where I had to go and heal the things that were keeping me from feeling alive. After the ceremony, I had a feeling there was something more waiting for me.

On our hike to Machu Picchu, Jesse encouraged us to spread out on the trail and spend time alone with ourselves. I stopped walking for a moment along the edge of a crystal clear mountain lake. I stood silently in this spot, soaking in nature's beauty. Suddenly it hit me. Out of nowhere the truth came to me in a gentle whisper: "I am good to my core. I am good!" I felt this light - it felt like coming out of a dark tunnel that I was stuck in for a very long time. I could feel the weight lift from my body. I felt so free. For the first time I felt free!

The work I did on your retreat opened me up to my truth. Now it's like seeing through clear eyes what is really true about myself and really was always there! Life's journey is continuously growing and getting better. I am so grateful for every moment.

— Briana

LOOKING FORWARD – NEXT STEPS

Dear Reader,

We have almost reached the end of our time together in this book.

But does it have to end here?

Maybe this is just the beginning.

The beginning of a new chapter.

A new chapter in your life

Your...Wild...&...Precious...Life

It's up to you...

Jesse

Your Own Life Is a Fierce Thing to Follow

I WILL LEAVE YOU WITH A POWERFUL PIECE of writing that has greatly informed my life. I hope it inspires you, as you journey onward into your Wild and Precious Life!

There is a way in which we should be eaten by life... that we should be absolutely consumed by it. There is nothing worse than getting to your deathbed and finding that you have been gummed to death! And you have never been able to give yourself over to the teeth of existence.

Because your own life...is a fierce thing to follow.

Because it's constantly leading you into larger and larger imaginative territories, for which you feel you are unprepared, and into which you enter almost as a child no matter what time in your life you've gotten to.

If you are truly following your life and your path, a part of you will always feel like you are a child in a new world. I think it's one of the great tasks especially around midlife to rehabilitate the innocence in your own body and your own vision of the world. To find the kind of wilder, youthful part of you that is actually undying.

If you feel the youthful part of you retreating away from you and you just accept it as a concomitant of growing older, it simply means that in a way you are getting used to things that

you shouldn't be getting used to. I think it gets harder as we get older, because you have to make constantly greater and greater sacrifices in order to stay closer to yourself. And you've got to keep giving things away until what is essential is just left to you.
— **David Whyte, English poet**

What's Available to You?

I F THIS BOOK HAS AWOKEN SOMETHING INSIDE YOU, there are several exciting ways for you to continue your journey...

Coaching

For one year, you and I work together to realize your meaningful and challenging project, focusing on both your *inner* and *outer* experience.

Most people have something really important that they have been putting off "until someday." Perhaps it's changing careers, writing a book or building a meaningful business. Maybe it's completing a relationship, starting a non-profit or finally getting out of a challenging rut.

It's the thing that you know you can't do alone. It's the thing that you are thinking about right now.

And... even if only half of you believes that your vision is possible, that's enough.

Reach out to me. I would love to hear about your vision, and see how I can support you.

Insight Adventures™

Join us this year for a unique, transformational life experience. We provide an opportunity to take time out of your daily routine to combine outdoor adventure and service with inner exploration. After returning home, you will receive coaching as a follow-up to create sustainable life change.

An excerpt from an email we received from a guest on a recent retreat to Nepal:

"A life-changer. That was my trip to Nepal with Jesse Gros. An intimate time spent with local people who know, revere and love Jesse - farmers, monks, students, orphans, guides. A multi-day trek to the summit of Edmund Hillary's favorite mountain, nights spent in farmhouses and monasteries, unforgettable encounters with lamas.

"Absolutely superb food and camp facilities en route. Organized and relaxed. An inner and outer journey that taught me about Love, Humility, Peace and Contentedness. The scenery is breathtaking - be it the hustle and bustle of Kathmandu, or the majestic Himalaya. If you like seeing lots of other tourists - this trip probably isn't for you. We hardly saw any. Local, less trodden paths are where Jesse takes you. It was perfect." — Roy Dunn

Go to **InsightAdventures.com** to view current trips and to request an application.

ABOUT JESSE GROS

Jesse Gros is a life coach, adventurer and healer. Through his one-on-one coaching, healing work and retreats, Jesse is a wayshower, guiding people to truly live their wild and precious lives.

Jesse is not only a force for change, he walks his talk. In 2009, in the midst of the economic recession, Jesse walked away from a lucrative professional career to follow his calling. Within four years he had created a thriving coaching and retreat business.

Jesse holds a Master's in Spiritual Psychology from the University of Santa Monica and is a Certified Life Coach, Breathwork Healer and TED Speaker Coach.

www.JesseGros.com

Made in the USA
San Bernardino, CA
16 May 2019